COWBOYS

THE END OF THE TRAIL

D0026880

By Alton Pryor

Stagecoach Publishing
5360 Campcreek Loop
Roseville, CA 95747
916-771-8166
stagecoach@surewest.net
www.stagecoachpublishng.com

COWBOYS

THE END OF THE TRAIL

Copyright 2005 by Alton Pryor
Library Congress Control Number: 2005900758

ISBN: 0-9747551-2-5

First Printing 2005
Second Printing 2006

Stagecoach Publishing
5360 Campcreek Loop
Roseville, CA. 95747
916-771-8166
Email: stagecoach@surewest.net
www.stagecoachpublishing.com

Introduction

'Nobody Counted Cowboys'

The cowboy entered the American picture out of necessity. There were things to do and he did them.

Describing the American cowboy is not an easy task, as he reached into the heart of so many people. In the minds of both the young and the old, the cowboy rivals Santa Claus. He instills good in everybody.

From my own experience, it looked like I would end up a farmer. That's what my dad and older brother did and fresh out of high school, that is what I did.

I literally hated it. I wanted to be a cowboy. After two years of farming, I decided to make the break. I got a job as the only all-around hand on a cattle ranch. While I savor the experience, it brought about an awakening.

From the very time he can talk, a youngster wants to be a cowboy. And that is good, for the cowboy is good. As most cowboys will admit, it is not the road to riches, but it is a rich road on which to travel.

Tracking the historic life of the cowboy is a difficult job. The American cowboy left few tracks. Historians find themselves dealing with an image rather than facts.

For instance, how many cowboys were out there roaming the range at any given time? How many were black, Mexican, Indian, or of any other ethnic character? **Nobody counted cowboys.**

Even a man who once worked as a cowboy and then went on to greater accomplishments, such as banking or other business ventures, will invariably label himself a "cowboy". To him, the "cowboy" label indicates greater accomplishment than do the more mundane business activities of the entrepreneur, whether it is banker, lawyer, or Congressman. It's "Once a cowboy, always a cowboy."

Acknowledgements

Some people have been very helpful in my getting this book assembled. First is my son, Scott, who has the impossible task of educating a thickheaded author in the vagaries of the computer. As though that is not calling enough, he was asked to read and also assist his father in formatting the book. We are especially indebted to Carolyn Hunter and the Texas Longhorn Breeders Association for the beautiful cover. Also, we want to thank Marilyn Demas for adding her proofreading and editing skills to the project. Vicky Kometani, current events coordinator for the Parker Ranch, searched for and found a photo that could be used with the chapter on the Hawaiian cowboys, or paniolos. We offer our thanks and gratitude to all. To those people we have omitted, it was unintentional, and believe me, we thank you too.

Alton Pryor

Table of Contents

Cover:
Courtesy Texas Longhorn Breeders Association of America. (Photo by Carolyn Hunter)

Chapter 1

The Vaquero

> *The horses introduced by Cortès were unlike those that are believed to have roamed Mexico and much of North America sixty million years earlier.*

The first cowboys spoke Spanish and called themselves vaqueros. They were the *charros* on the brushy hillsides of what is now Mexico.

They learned their craft by riding horses that were descendants of animals introduced by the Spanish conquistadors in the 16th century.

The first cattle were longhorns, brought by Spaniards in 1534. The vaqueros developed their skills and the language that would live on through the American cowboy. They developed their skills in the haciendas of colonial Mexico.

This new breed of worker differed greatly from the vaqueros of old Spain, who generally herded docile cows on foot. These new vaqueros were horsemen first and foremost.

The vaqueros were skilled riders who worked with wild and dangerous animals and faced serious harm or even death on a daily basis. And they were adamant about their positions, disdaining work that could not be done from a saddle.

In the deserts of northern Mexico a man on foot was of little value. The vaqueros took great pride in their horsemanship abilities. Even though poor, their horsemanship gave them a sense of power and pride that their poor brethren had never known.

Spanish vaquero as painted by Frederic Remington.

He was particularly proud of his skill with a rope, and firmly believed he could ride any horse that lived. This loyalty and pride passed down to the American cowboy.

The language of the charros penetrated and was adopted by American cowboys. Words such as rodeo, buckaroo, lariat, and other terms became and still are common language for American cowboys.

The vaquero crafted a legacy of skills, language and style that would live on in the cowboy, who would become perhaps the most beloved character in all of history.

Hernàn Cortès, a young Spanish lawyer, set out to conquer New Spain (Mexico). It is believed by some historians that Cortès would not have been successful in defeating New Spain and the Mexican Indians if it weren't for the horses used by his cavalry.

The "Big Dogs" used by Cortès and his army frightened the Mexican Indians. They had never seen horses before and believed that man and beast were one. The frightened Indians offered little resistance to the "man-horse" army.

California vaqueros amused themselves by roping a bull and throwing the animal to the ground. Courtesy California Historical Society

When Cortès landed at Vera Cruz in 1519, he brought with him sixteen Spanish horses, including eleven stallions and five mares. Ironically, the Spaniards were unaware they had just introduced horses to a continent where the species may have originated and then vanished.

The horses reintroduced by Cortès were unlike those that roamed Mexico and much of North America sixty million years earlier. Some writers say the horses brought by Cortès were of Arabian stock, but they were Andalusian.

Another Spaniard, Gregorio de Villalobos introduced cattle to New Spain. Within a few years, cattle became plentiful there. The Spaniards let most of their cattle wander at will, but the Aztec Indian farmers soon complained that animals were trampling on their maize and other crops.

Many of these animals were not branded, and Spaniards often rounded up these strays and branded them as their own.

15

This practice became known as "mavericking," first in Texas and then elsewhere in the American west.

In an effort to keep peace, the city council ordered the establishment of a local stockmen's organization called the *Mesta*. The Mesta was to become the model of all organized stockmen's groups in the Western Hemisphere.

The town council ordered that "there shall be two judges of the Mesta in the city who shall twice annually call together all stockmen who should make it known if they had any stray animals in their herds."

Further, each stockowner was directed to identify all his animals with his own brand. These brands were registered in what most probably was the first brand book in the Western Hemisphere. The book was kept at Mexico City.

Ear cropping of cattle for identification was forbidden by the Mesta code of 1537. It was felt that such marks could be easily changed and were viewed as an invitation to fraud and deception.

The Mesta also regulated the number and size of dogs a sheepman could have. The directive ordered that sheepmen could have only mastiffs, large dogs with short fawn-colored coats.

The Mesta, for all intents and purposes, became a cattlemen's protective association, similar to the ones that come into being in the American West.

Chapter 2

Hoboes on Horseback

> *The cowboy slept on a "Tucson bed"*
> *which he made by lying on his stomach*
> *and covering it with his back.*

This is a side of the cowboy's story that is difficult to tell. The image of the cowboy is the most romantic and longest lasting mythic image to come out of America. This image is believed to have originated with the pulp magazines that were popular in the 1870s.

These magazines portrayed the cowboy as bigger than life, typifying virility, action, excitement, freedom, loyalty, independence, determination and above all, competence.

Adding to the romance of the cowboy was Owen Wister, author of *The Virginian.* Wister and his predecessor James Fenimore Cooper (1789-1851) created the basic western myths and themes, which were later popularized by such writers as Zane Grey and Max Brand.

In 1885, at the age of 25, author Owen Wister came west for his health. For several years he kept a full and realistic account of his Western experiences in a series of private diaries. Those experiences provided him with much of the material used in the first Western novel ever written.

"The Virginian" which was published in 1902, made a legendary hero of the cowboy, immortalized the Town of Medicine Bow, and put the phrase "When You Call Me That, Smile," into the American language.

In reality, the epic years of the cowboy ran from 1866, when the first longhorns crossed the Red River into Indian Territory, until 1897, when John McCanless pushed the last herd north on one of the Texas trails.

Cowboy and his horse take a break.
(National Geographic)

Writing in *This is the West,* a book with a collection of writers about western history, Charles W. Towne said, "In those thirty years, there were probably never more than twenty five thousand 'working cowboys' on the plains in any one year."

The author added, "They constituted one of the most motley collections of dare-devils ever assembled."

There were veterans who had starved during the last days at Appomattox with Lee, second sons of English nobility, Negroes new to freedom, steamboat gamblers "on the lam", overland freighters, farm boys running away from home, Mexican vaqueros and half-breed *comancheros.*

According to Towne, the word "Cowboy" first appeared in the English language on the big cattle ranches of Ireland about one thousand A.D.

The term cowboy may have been introduced to New England around 1640 by Irish prisoners of war. It is known that the leather-jerkined herdsmen that drove John Pynchon's first herd of stall-fattened beeves from Springfield to Boston, Massachusetts were called "cowboys" During the American Revolution, cattle thieves and raiders that favored the British were also referred to as "cowboys".

The world's love affair with the American cowboy blossomed in the nineteenth century and has never stopped blooming since. Artists, too, have contributed to the love affair. Frederic Remington and Charles Russell have painted the cowboy as the hero in virtually every situation one can imagine.

The cowboy that participated in the trail drives out of Texas to northern markets was not the six-gun-toting, hard-riding bronc-buster that always wins the girl type of man. Cowboys tended to be young men looking for escapes in life. Many lads chose to become cowboys because their other choice would have been following a plow.

Cowboys of all races marched the giant herds from Texas to the northern markets.   (Prints and Photographs Division, Library of Congress)

Most were poorly educated or even illiterate, but they often learned the alphabet by learning to read cattle brands. Some cowboys had prodigious memories and could recognize a brand and to whom it belonged.

Those who were better schooled were not satisfied with being just a cowboy. They moved into the higher ranks of the cattle business by building their own ranches and herds.

A trail drive wasn't as adventurous as most young cowboys expected. When young Jimmy Cook hired on with Charlie Slaughter in the 1870s, he got a briefing from Joe Roberts, the trail boss:

"They tell us you can catch a cow and can shoot a rabbits eye out at every pop. Now, if you can ride for the next four months without a whole night's sleep, and turn your gun loose on any damned Injun that tries to get our horses, well, get ready. We roll out tomorrow."

Jimmy Cook later told of the accommodations he had on the trail. "The bed, when you get a chance to hit it, was the bare ground. A Tucson-bed," he explained, "is made by lying on your stomach and covering that with your back. It was allowable to put your saddle and saddle blanket over your head as protection from any hailstones larger than hen's eggs."

It is evident in that one, or at most two, trail drives provided the cowboy with all the adventure he needed. He seldom signed on for another trek across the plains.

One cowboy who found a better way was James Emmit McCauley, a Texas cowboy.

"I have done as most cowpunchers do after they have got too stove up to ride. For a man to be stove up at thirty may sound strange to some people, but many a cowboy has been so bunged up that he has quit riding early in life.

"Now at thirty I went back to my early raising. When I realized I could no longer follow the long-horned cattle I determined not to work for wages any longer. In just a little less than a month after I left the hospital I had married a girl I had known 10 years or longer. I found my little capital had went down until I was worth less than $500.

"I've been married now three years and I have 320 acres of land and it would take $5,000 to get me to move. I consider I have done better than I possibly could have done working for wages."

During a stampede, riders could hear the horns of the longhorns clash.
(The Longhorns, by J. Frank Dobie)

A man on horseback could look at the horizon and make a living at least as good as the man following a mule. Roping and working cattle on horseback was simply a better and more exciting way of life than chopping weeds and picking cotton.

Most cowhands were southwestern boys from Texas or Louisiana. Many had been soldiers in the Civil War, and some were attempting to hide a past. While most were white, there were a number of black cowboys, Mexicans and Indians who participated in the cattle drives to the northern markets.

One rancher described his hiring practices thusly, "We take a man here and ask no questions. We know when he throws a saddle on his horse whether he understands his business or not."

The home for the cowboy during the winter was often a line shack in a remote portion of the cattle range. Most of them had a "good luck" horseshoe over the door.   *(Erwin E. Smith Collection, Amon Carter Museum, Fort Worth)*

Teddy Blue Abbott rode with a cattle drive in 1879. "The Olives (Print Olive, a Texas rancher) was (sic) mostly hard on Mexicans and Negroes because being from Texas they was (sic) born and raised with that intense hatred of a Mexican, and being Southern, free black men was (sic) poison to them. But they hired them because they worked cheaper than white men."

In the succession of things on the range, cattle replaced buffalo and cowboys replaced Indians. There are some that say it was the cattlemen that led to the demise of the buffalo on the range. But Robert V. Hine and John Mack Faragher, authors of *The American West, a new interpretive history*, disagree.

"Although cattlemen profited from the elimination of the great buffalo herds, they had little to do with the work of destruction. That was something accomplished by buffalo hide hunters, aided and abetted by the frontier army and General Sherman himself."

In truth, the cowboys who participated in the cattle drive were literally "hoboes on horseback", or, as some would call them, "drifters". They had no home, and the only thing they owned was their riding equipment, which they themselves had to furnish in order to get a job with a cow outfit. They didn't even own the horses they used on the job.

Herding cows was seasonal work, with spring and fall roundups the busy times. Consequently, cowboys were mobile and trekked from job to job.

To suggest that the cowboy was little more than a common tramp or hobo simply doesn't fit the image that has been painted. The cowboy's public image may be the true reason historians have been reticent to document the actual history of the cowboy's life. Nobody wants to spoil the image.

The image of the cowboy as being strong and true did hold forth in a lot of areas. For instance, deals for thousands of dollars worth of cattle or horses might be sealed by nothing more than a handshake.

The cowboy in history, and historians agree on this, was often a reckless fellow. William Savage, in his book the *The Cowboy Hero*, says, "Indeed the very word 'cowboy' has become synonymous with recklessness.

After three months on the trail, the cowboy was ready to celebrate. He had just drawn his pay, which meant he had about one hundred dollars in his jeans, and that money was burning a hole in his pocket. He was ready for entertainment, or to put it more bluntly, to be entertained.

It wasn't unusual for a cowboy to have his first sexual experience in one of the highflying trail towns, such as Abilene, Kansas. Too, often, the only woman a cowboy might know would

A mountain of buffalo bones c. 1880.
(Burton Historical Collection, Detroit Public Library)

be one of the "soiled doves" who set up her shop in a cattle trail town.

Cowboys probably got their reputation for being wild by frequenting the cattle town "demimonde". These towns were no different from the towns of the gold rush in attracting whiskey peddlers, gamblers, and the ever-anticipated dance hall ladies.

Joseph Snell reportedly tracked the history of more than six hundred cattle town prostitutes who turned tricks from 1870 to 1885. Like the cowboys themselves, they were young (average age twenty three). "Prostitution was a melting pot where the only general criterion was possession of a female body," said Snell.

Little is known about what homosexual activity occurred among cowboys in the cow camps, where circumstance dictated that males associated only with other males. The word, "homosexual", was not coined until the 1890s. Whatever might have gone on at night stayed out there under the stars.

Roping a longhorn
(National Geographic)

Some cowhands did get into gunfights, some with severe consequences, as told by this epitaph: *Here lies Les Moore. Shot by a .44. No Les. No Moore.*

In 1867, the Kansas Pacific Railroad established a stockyard and depot in Abilene, Kansas. Some reports say that Texas cattlemen trailed 35,000 beef cattle to the railhead that year. Cattle soon became one of the most important cargoes of the railroads.

Edward C. Abbott was born in Cranwich, England, and was brought to the west by his parents as a boy. His father hoped the open air would improve Teddy Abbott's frail health. He allowed Teddy to help drive a herd of cattle from Texas to Nebraska

25

when he was just 10 years old. The experience, Abbott said later, "made a cowboy out of me. Nothing could have changed me after that."

A longhorn herd of two thousand steers would require ten to fifteen or more cowboys. The drive would need a *remuda* of 100 to 150 horses from which cowboys could select a new mount each day.

On one drive, where a cattle stampede occurred, a cowboy told his boss, "I'm going to Greenland where the nights are six months long, and I ain't going to get up until ten o'clock the next day."

In the book, *We Headed Them North*, Abbott recalled the dust was thick as fur on the eyebrows of the drag men during a cattle drive. "They coughed up black phlegm for weeks," He said. "There were days of deadly dull work punctuated by moments of high drama, when sudden stampedes of hundreds of steers, dry runs with animals bellowing from thirst, and infernal weather."

After his first trail drive, Teddy Blue Abbott bought a fancy shirt and pants, a white Stetson, and hand-tooled boots. "Lord I was proud of those clothes!" he remembered. When he arrived home in Nebraska, his sister took one look at him and declared, "Take your pants out of your boots and put your coat on. You look like an outlaw!"

Cowboys earned thirty or forty dollars a month. It is fairly plain that nobody became a cowboy to get rich. The most likely attraction was because of a lad's affection for horses. It wasn't the cow that cowboys loved, it was generally his association with the horse he rode.

Today, the cowboy profession, outside of the "rodeo" cowboys, is virtually finished. The few who still work the cattle often do so from the seat of a sturdy pickup truck rather than from the back of a horse. Present-day equipment allows six cowboys to brand more than fifty head of cattle in an hour.

In his book, *Visions of the American West*, Gerald F. Kreyche wrote: "Today, being a cowboy is more an attitude than an occupation." That statement may be too close to the truth to give comfort to those few cowboys holding onto the image.

There is a verse in "The Old Chisholm Trail" that may fall near to the truth:

When I got to the boss and tried to draw my roll,
He had me figured out nine dollars in the hole.
I'll sell my outfit as soon as I can
And I wouldn't punch cows for no damned man

Chapter 3

The Texas Longhorns

> A century or so of running wild made the
> longhorns tough and hardy enough to
> withstand blizzards, droughts, dust storms,
> attacks by other animals, and Indians.

The Texas Longhorn is as much a part of the cowboy's history as the cowboy himself.

These are the animals brought to the Americas by Christopher Columbus more than 500 years ago. They first arrived in America in the form of Spanish *retinto* (criollo) cattle.

The first Anglo-American settlers of Texas came to raise cotton. However, they brought with them a few cows, mostly of northern European breeds. These cows mixed with the Spanish breeds already in Texas and soon grew into considerable herds. Most of the cattle for the first stocking of the central and northern plains came from these herds.

As the number of cattle increased in Texas, small acreage owners ranged their cattle primarily upon unoccupied public lands. In fact, some cattle owners with thousands of head of cattle did not even own one acre of land.

Other men who moved to Texas invested all their capital in cattle and then depended on the open range for pasture. Some of those with no capital got their start by branding calves "on share" for others. At that time men were employed to brand calves and they received one calf out of every four branded "on share."

The Texas Longhorn became the foundation of the American cattle industry. In 1690, the first herd of cattle, only about 200 head, was driven northward from Mexico to a mission near the

Sabine River, a land that would become known as Texas. The early missions and ranchers would not survive all of the elements. But the Texas Longhorn would. A century or so of running wild made the longhorns tough and hardy enough to withstand blizzards, droughts, dust storms, attacks by other animals, and Indians.

They did not require great amounts of water to survive. Their horns served for attack and defense. A strong sense of smell made it easy for a cow to find her calf and she would ferociously defend this calf.

By the time of the Civil War, nearly 300 years after setting foot in America, millions of longhorns ranged between the mesquite-dotted sandy banks of the Rio Bravo to the sand beds of the Sabine.

Texas drovers took one of these trails to get their cattle to northern markets.
(From the book, *The Wild West*)

Most of the longhorns were the unbranded survivors of Indian raids, stampedes and bad weather. Some escaped from missions or were abandoned after ranch failures.

The survivors of the Civil War returned home to Texas to find abandoned ranches, unplowed farm fields—and herds of wild cattle, which would soon become gold in their pockets. In the next quarter century, 10 million head were trailed north to fatten on lush midwestern grasses or shipped directly by rail to the beef-hungry East.

Mother Nature groomed longhorns. They carried the ideal characteristics of resistance. They could go incredible distances without water, rustle their own food, fend for themselves, swim rivers, and survive the desert sun and winter snow. Therefore, they were tremendous for long drives.

There was probably no meaner creature in Texas than a longhorn bull. The slightest provocation would turn him into an aggressive and dangerous enemy. The bull's horns usually measured about six feet from tip-to-tip, but could measure over eight feet long. In addition, the sharpness of horns of any length, the speed and muscle power of the bull, and the ease with which he could be aroused and enraged, made him a dangerous and uncontrollable animal. When two bulls met, there was sure to be a fight, often to death. And only a very well armed cowboy had a chance against a longhorn bull.

Western historian J. Frank Dobie wrote in the *Fort Worth Press* in 1936, "There is a widespread idea, even among people who should know better, that trail driving originated after the Civil War, when a lone Texas herd headed for some vague point 'north of 36.'

"As a matter of fact, on the very day the Texans whipped the Mexicans at San Jacinto, in 1836, a herd of Texas Longhorns from Taylor White's ranch west of the Neches River was trailing for New Orleans.

"Cattle had been trailed out of Texas before that. Through the 'forties they were trailed north into Missouri and also to Louisiana markets. There is a record of one herd's trailing to New York, about 1850, and through the 'fifties thousands of steers were driven across the continent to California. The trailing business attained volume and became well organized when in 1867 Abilene, Kansas, opened as a market."

Translating wild cattle into hard cash was an epic struggle between man, beast and the elements—from this grew the romantic legends of the Western Cowboy.

In 1927 Will C. Barnes and other Forest Service men saved the Texas Longhorn from probable extinction, when they collected a small herd of breeding stock in South Texas for the Wichita Mountains Wildlife Refuge in Oklahoma.

A few years later western writer J. Frank Dobie, with the help of former range inspector Graves Peeler and financial support from oilman Sid W. Richardson, gathered small herds for Texas state parks.

After the wildlife-refuge herd had increased to several hundred, the Forest Service held annual sales of surplus animals. Cowmen at first purchased them as curiosities, then rediscovered the longhorn's longevity, resistance to disease, fertility, ease of calving, and ability to thrive on marginal pastures. Its growing popularity in beef herds was spurred by a diet-conscious population's desire for lean beef.

Chapter 4

The American Cowboy

> *Morally, as a class, cowboys are foulmouthed, blasphemous, drunken, lecherous, and utterly corrupt. Usually harmless on the plains when sober, they are dreaded in towns, for then liquor has an ascendancy over them.*
>
> Cheyenne Daily Leader

The cowboy may be the most emulated character in all of American history, yet his past remains hidden from view. We may know what he did, but we really don't know who he was.

Charles Goodnight, in later years

Yet the cowboy era had greatness about it, a greatness of spirit that was as much a part of the cowboy as the cowboy was a part of his times.

Nobody personified the role that became known as the American Cowboy more than Charlie Goodnight. Yet, despite his scant education, a daring idea and the determination to make it succeed helped Charles Goodnight become one of the west's most prosperous and respected cattlemen.

Goodnight moved from Illinois to Texas at the age of ten with his mother and stepfather. At age 21, Goodnight and his stepbrother Wes Sheek were urged to take over a herd

The first Spanish longhorns brought to the U.S. from Mexico were black. The most famous of these was Charles Goodnight's "Old Blue," a born herd leader.

(Buffalo Bill Historical Center, Cody, Wyoming)

of four hundred cows by Clinton Varney, a wealthy businessman in Waco. Varney was Sheek's brother-in-law.Under the arrangement, Goodnight and Sheek would receive every fourth calf as their pay.

Cows and calves were generally not salable, and steers couldn't be marketed until the animals were four or five years old. This meant that Charlie and Wes could not expect any early profits until these young calves reached a salable age four or five years later. Grass was cheap. They could graze the animals wherever they pleased. They chose the Keechi Valley in Palo Pinto County.

Goodnight answered a call for volunteers to join the regiment of Minute Men for a campaign against the Comanches and Kiowas who were marauding the cattle herds developing near the Indian Nations. He later joined the Texas Rangers where he became a scout.

His duties with the Rangers kept him away from the Keechi Valley for weeks at a time, but during his absence, his stepbrother Wes Sheek kept the operation together. Times were bad, however, and Confederate currency was hardly worth anything.

Over a period of time, Charlie developed an idea. His plan was modeled after a cattle drive that Oliver Loving had made to market cattle in Denver, where a gold rush was creating a demand for beef. No one was more impressed with Loving's success than Charlie Goodnight.

Instead of taking the shortest way to Denver, which would mean traveling through Comanche and Kiowa country, where he was likely to lose everything, Charlie decided to take a longer route, adding several hundred miles of extra trail driving to his task.

Goodnight called on Oliver Loving for his advice. Loving approved of the route Charlie proposed to get around the Comanche and Kiowa territory, even though it meant traveling six days without water at one point. Loving approved of Charlie's plan.

"He called me Charlie, but in my respect for him I always addressed him as Mr. Loving. I don't believe I ever called him Oliver," Goodnight recalled years later. "As we talked, he pointed out the difficulties I was likely to face. I refused to be discouraged, and after we had talked for some time, he said, to my surprise, 'If you will let me, I will go with you.'

"'I will not only let you,' I told him, 'but it's the most desirable thing of my life. I not only need the assistance of you and your crew, I need your advice.'"

Goodnight's and Loving's names would forever be a part of history following their epic undertaking. They threw their herds together southwest of Belknap, Texas for the beginning of their historic drive.

With them were 18 men, including a man known as "One-armed Bill Wilson," who was known to be a top hand in any outfit even though he lacked one limb.

Charlie Goodnight

Goodnight and Loving knew they faced trouble when they camped for the second night. The cows were both thirsty and hungry and refused to bed down. Their milling throughout the night kept the cowboys in their saddles and there was no rest that night.

Two hours before dawn, Goodnight put the herd back on the trail with a plan to drive them straight through without stopping.

In their weakened condition, and frantic for water, the herd refused to be hazed forward. By noon, the cowboys had gotten the herd strung out for two miles as Goodnight and Wilson tried to hold back the leaders and allow the stragglers to catch up.

Oliver Loving was working the drag. He was trying to cope with the straggling herd. Eventually he had to leave more than three hundred cows behind, many of them with calves at their sides. The calves would perish on the spot.

Goodnight, who had scouted ahead to the Pecos River the previous day, spotted a pond of stagnant, alkali-laden water that was poisonous to both man and beast. It would be death to the herd if the cowboys couldn't force the cattle around it.

The trail drivers accomplished the task and forged on toward the Pecos River. When the herd did reach the Pecos, the trough of the river was ten feet below the precipitous bank. Instead of stopping, the pressure from the rear cattle forced the leaders to plunge over the bank to the river 10 feet below.

The river was at its lowest ebb, however, and in a few minutes the river channel was filled with a mass of crazed, struggling cattle. Many were pushed out onto the western bank of the river without a chance to drink.

To make matters worse, there were quick sands above the crossing, and some of the cattle that escaped the crush of the onrushing herd were sucked under

It was a sad moment when Goodnight conducted a tally of the remaining herd. He figured that half of the two thousand cattle that began the drive were lost. Later summing up the situation, Goodnight called it "the graveyard of a cowman's hopes."

Goodnight and Loving rested the cattle and horses for three days before striking out again. A scouting trip had revealed that some grass was available about twenty miles up on the eastern bank of the Pecos. One-Armed Bill Wilson later described the area as "damned little grass and a million rattlesnakes."

As they traveled north up the river, both the grass and the palatability of the Pecos improved. The cowboys, however, every morning found newly born calves on the bedding grounds.

These newborns had to be shot and left for the coyotes, as the calves would not be able to keep up with the herd.

The trail drivers had no specific destination in mind until they were within forty miles of Fort Sumner.* The Army had some eight thousand Navajos and Mesaleros confined in the Bosque Redondo (Round Timbers) Reservation.

To make matters brighter for Goodnight and Loving, they were having trouble feeding the Indians. The situation had grown so dire the government contractors paid as high as sixteen cents a pound for beef.

Goodnight hurried ahead to take advantage of this bonanza. Goodnight got eight cents a pound on the hoof. The Fort Sumner contractors refused to buy the stock cattle in the herd, leaving Goodnight and Loving with some seven or eight hundred cows and year-old calves.

The cowboys drove these animals north to Las Carretas Creek to rest, while the owners celebrated their good fortune and counted their money.

While Loving was considered well to do, Charlie Goodnight had never had so much money. His share was $12,000. The money he made instilled a thirst in him for even more. He wanted to return at once to Texas and bring another herd to Horsehead Crossing for another bonanza.

It was decided Loving would go on to Colorado and dispose of the cows and calves. The plan called for Loving and Goodnight to meet at a spot on the lower Pecos later in the fall.

Goodnight then began the seven hundred mile return trip, accompanied by three of his best men. In his saddlebags he carried the gold he had received for first trail drive. He and his men rode mules on the return trip because of their staying power. In case of attack, each man led a horse for a quick getaway.

*Fort Sumner was later abandoned as a fort and became famous as the place where Sheriff Pat Garrett killed William Bonney, known as "Billy the Kid" on July 14, 1881.

37

Playing cards, such as a game of hearts that being played here, was one way to relieve the boredom. (Amon Carter Museum, Fort Worth)

With a herd of some fifteen hundred three-and-four-year-old steers, Goodnight started a second drive in September. Using the knowledge they had gained from the first trip, the trail herders laid up during the hot hours of the day and traveled at night.

Goodnight and his cowboys found Loving and his crew at the agreed upon rendezvous. Because of impending weather, Fort Sumner and Santa Fe were beyond reach before winter set in.

The cowboys trailed the cattle to Bosque Grande, instead, and turned the animals out on grass for the winter. The cowboys, meanwhile, built dugouts and harvested firewood to keep them warm during the months of waiting.

The trail drivers had demonstrated the practicality of their trail. And in 1868, Goodnight extended the Goodnight-Loving Trail by driving all the way to Wyoming, and later on, into Montana. It came to be called the Texas Trail.

Charlie Goodnight was one cowboy that did count in cowboy history. When asked for an opinion of Goodnight, John Chisum sometimes called "The Cattle King of America" during the 1800s, answered, "He knows cow."

Chapter 5

Arbuckles' Cowboy Coffee

> **Arbuckle's Coffee**
> *Upon hearing the cook's call "Who wants the candy?" some of the toughest Cowboys on the trail were known to die for the opportunity of manning the coffee grinder in exchange for satisfying a sweet tooth.*

A cowboy just couldn't start his day without that wakeup with a strong cup of coffee. Whether at the ranch or on a cattle drive, that coffee was generally strong enough to float a horseshoe.

Until the end of the Civil War, coffee was sold green. It was up to the ranch cook or the chuck wagon cook to roast the beans on a wood stove or in a skillet over a campfire. This was no easy chore, for one burned bean ruined the whole batch.

Ranch and trail cooks must have issued a sigh of relief when John Arbuckle announced in 1865 that he and his brother Charles were patenting a coffee roasting process that would eliminate the need for roasting.

Improvement in Roasted Coffee.

To all whom it may concern:

Be it known that I, John Arbuckle, Jr., of the city and county of Allegheny, in the State of Pennsylvania, have invented a new and useful Improvement in "Roasted Coffee;" and I do hereby declare that the following is a full and exact description thereof.

The nature of my invention consists in roasting coffee and then coating it with a glutinous or gelatinous matter, for the purpose of retaining the aroma of the coffee, and also act as a clarifying-agent when the ground coffee has been boiled in water.

To enable others skilled in the art of "roasting coffee" to use my invention, I will proceed to describe its operation or preparation.

I take any good article of green coffee, and roast it by any of the known means. I then cool it as quickly as possible. I then prepare a mixture of the following ingredients, in about the following proportions: One ounce of Irish moss; half an ounce of isinglass; half an ounce of gelatine; one ounce of white sugar; and twenty-four eggs.

I boil the Irish moss in a quart of water, and then strain it. I then boil the isinglass and gelatine in a pint of water. I then mix the sugar and eggs well together, and when the mixture of Irish moss, isinglass, gelatine, and water has become cold, I mix the whole of the ingredients into one homogenous compound.

I then pour the whole over about one hundred pounds of the roasted coffee, and stir and so manipulate the coffee that each grain will be entirely coated, after the coffee is coated, and the coating has become dry and hard, which is accomplished by forcing currents of air through it while stirring it, for the purpose of coating it with the glutinous or gelatinous matter described.

(Signed) John Arbuckle

Arbuckle coffee thus became a staple of the ranch and camp cook. Marketed under the name ARBUCKLES' ARIOSA COFFEE, in patented, airtight, one pound packages, the new coffee was an instant success with chuck wagon cooks in the west whose responsibility was keeping cowboys supplied with plenty of hot coffee out on the range.

The patented process included roasting and coating the coffee beans with an egg and sugar glaze to hold in the coffee flavor and aroma of the newly roasted beans. Arbuckle's coffee was distributed in the age before lined paper bags, and coffee went stale and rancid pronto.

Coating, or "glazing" as it came to be known, was a way to lengthen its shelf life by keeping air away from the beans. Many different compounds were used in the coffee trade. Arbuckle Bros. settled on a sugar-based glaze.

They became such a prodigious user of sugar that they decided to enter the sugar business rather than give a profit on the huge quantities they needed.

The Sugar Trust didn't like that much and decided to enter the coffee business to spite Arbuckle. For the better part of the next generation, the Sugar Trust's LION COFFEE battled it out with Arbuckle's brands throughout the courts and the cities of the nation. The first great advertising campaign in history was this coffee war.

After fighting to a standstill, the sugar boys quit the coffee business, and the Arbuckle brothers were triumphant. They strode upon the national stage until their deaths in the early part of the 20th Century.

ARBUCKLES' ARIOSA COFFEE packages bore a yellow label with the name ARBUCKLES' in large red letters across the front, beneath which flew a flying Angel trademark over the words ARIOSA COFFEE in black letters.

The coffee was shipped all over the country in sturdy wooden crates, one hundred packages to a crate. ARBUCKLES' ARIOSA COFFEE became so dominant, particularly in the west, that many Cowboys were not aware there was any other kind. With keen marketing minds, the Arbuckle Brothers printed signature coupons on the bags of coffee redeemable for all manner of notions including handkerchiefs, razors, scissors, and wedding rings.

To sweeten the deal, each package of ARBUCKLES' contained a stick of peppermint candy. This allowed the chuck wagon cook to offer an incentive to a cowboy to grind a fresh supply of coffee. The cowboy doing the grinding got the peppermint stick.

Upon hearing the cook's call, 'Who wants the candy?' some of the toughest cowboys on the trail were known to vie for the opportunity of manning the coffee grinder in exchange for satisfying a sweet tooth.

Arbuckle Bros. produced ARIOSA, known as "the coffee that won the West," and also roasted and packed several other popular brands, including their premium YUBAN brand, which was the best selling brand in New York for years.

Mr. John Arbuckle, who went on to become the greatest coffee roaster of his generation was also one of the richest men in America during the gilded age of the 1880s and '90s.

Chapter 6

The Chuck Wagon

'You didn't see any fat cowboys'

> Only a fool argues with a skunk, a mule or a
> cook.   Kenny Trowbridge

The era of the western trail drives lasted only about 20 years, from the end of the Civil War until the mid-1880s.

To facilitate the feeding of his cowboys on the trail, Charles Goodnight, who helped found the Goodnight-Loving Trail, came up with the idea for a supply wagon that would not only carry the essential trail needs but serve as a working kitchen for the trail cook.

Frustrated by the inefficiency of transporting food and supplies for trail crews by the traditional methods of ox carts or pack horse, Goodnight obtained a surplus army wagon, stripped it down to its running gear, then transformed it into a mobile kitchen.

Goodnight called his new contraption a *chuck wagon*. He chose an army surplus Studebaker wagon for the basis of his invention. This wagon, with its steel axles, he figured, could withstand the grueling five month drives that often occurred in moving cattle up the long trails to market.

The cattleman then added a chuck box and a boot to the rear of the wagon. His design eventually became the prototype for all the chuck wagons that followed.

In the chuck box itself, Goodnight built a number of shelves and drawers that would keep supplies handy for the cook, and would keep them in good condition while traveling the bumpy trails from one camp to another.

45

A chuck wagon cook tends to business.
Amon Carter Museum, Fort Worth

The hinged lid that formed a door for the food supplies in the chuck box dropped down when in camp to provide a worktable for the cook. Attached to the side of the wagon was a water barrel large enough for two days' water supply.

An assortment of tool and catchall boxes was attached to the side of the wagon to hold a variety of supplies, including the ever-present coffee grinder. A canvas sling was placed underneath the wagon for stowing any precious wood the cook might see while moving from camp to camp.

Besides serving as the cook's traveling kitchen and the cowboy's home on long trail drives, the chuck wagon carried provisions for the trail hands, plus bedrolls, shovels, axes, rope, and even a few personal items.

Cowboys seldom ate meals at a table. While on the trail, they ate on whatever was handy. (National Archives, Washington, D.C.)

In the mid-1880's, when trail-driving reached its zenith and cattle ranching reached the vast open range of the 'Great Plains', market demand led the Studebaker Bros. Mfg. Co. of South Bend, Ind. to produce their 'Round-Up Wagon', especially designed for feeding large crews.

The Round-Up Wagon was heavier and less mobile than the lighter trail models.

During the long drives, the chuck wagon was the headquarters. Cowboys ate their meals there, and when not on duty, gathered there. It was the cowboy's social center, where tall tales, talk of the day's experiences, and just plain "windies" were told.

The cowboys held a lot of respect for the cook even though they didn't always enjoy his food. The cook ruled the wagon and wagon area with an absolute hand. His authority went unquestioned.

Wagon cooks had a reputation for being ill tempered. Their disposition may have been caused by the fact that his job required that he get up several hours before the men, and work later after the men bedded down.

When the campsite was moved, the cook had to be up and off ahead of the cattle, and he had to have a hot meal ready when the cattle arrived at the new campsite.

It was the cook who was the barber, the doctor, the banker, and sometimes the mediator if a disturbance arose among the cowboys.

There were some unwritten rules that were in force around the chuck wagon area. When cowboys approached the chuck wagon, they were expected to do it from downwind so that dusty didn't blow into the food.

No horse was to be tied to the chuck wagon's wheel or hobbled too close to camp. Cowboys didn't crowd around the cook's fire seeking warmth. Likewise, there was no scuffling or kicking up dust around the chuck wagon while meals were being served.

The cowboy had better not help himself to food or touch a cooking tool without the cook's permission. And one thing a cowboy surely didn't want to do was use the cook's worktable as a dining table.

After dishing food from a pot, the lid was placed where it wouldn't touch the dirt. And, it was poor manners to take the last piece of anything unless the rest of the group was through eating.

When a cowboy refilled his coffee cup during a meal, it was common for others to yell, "Man at the pot," which meant he was to refill their cups as well.

Author's Note: We have gone to a number of sources looking for authentic recipes as the trail cooks themselves might have prepared them. We can't always verify their authenticity, however.

Most dishes the chuck wagon cook made differed with each cooking, depending on the supplies on hand. For instance, there are at least a dozen recipes for "Son of a Bitch Stew" and each would be a little different. Where one cook would use kidneys, another would not. One liked using the spleen, and another left it out. Some liked onions, others dashes of chili pepper.

Son Of A Bitch Stew

1/2 the heart
1/2 the spleen
1/4 the liver
All the tongue
All the sweetbreads
Marrow gut (about 3 feet)
All the butcher's steak (the strips of lean meat on the inner side of the ribs), or an equal amount of tenderloin.
2 cups melted leaf fat
One set of brains

After the calf was killed and while the meat was still warm, the heart, liver, tongue, marrow gut, some pieces of tenderloin, or butcher's steak, sweetbreads and the brains were taken to be prepared. The cook cut the fat into small chunks, put them into the pot. While this fat was being melted he cut the heart into small cubes, adding it first because it was tougher. The tongue was also skinned and cubed, then added, thus giving the two toughest ingredients longer cooking time.

While these were cooking, the cook cut the tenderloin, sweetbreads and liver into similar pieces, using the liver sparingly so as not to make the stew bitter. To all this was added the marrow gut after being cut into rings, or inch long pieces. Cover all this with lukewarm water, adding more from time to time.

Mountain Oysters

Mountain Oysters, also known as prairie oysters, are that part of the male animal which is removed in his youth that he may thereby be more tractable and less, uh, masculine. They are considered to be quite a delicacy. Some butcher shops sell bull testicles. These are good but the best source is from young animals. The preparation of mountain oysters is quite simple:

Ingredients

    mountain oysters
    flour
    salt
    pepper
    paprika
    garlic
    cayenne

Preparation

Season the flour with the salt, pepper, paprika, garlic, and Cayenne. If the mountain oysters are large, cut them into bite sized chunks.

Dust the mountain oysters in the flour and sauté in a pan of hot oil or deep fry. They should be tender on the inside and crisp on the outside. Serve with horseradish sauce or cocktail sauce

Sour Dough Biscuits

One of the most important items in making and keeping Sour Dough Biscuits going is a proper container for the "starter," the best one being an earthenware crock with a good lid, close fitting but not air tight. DO NOT use a tin container, which can cause the dough to become toxic.

Directions

1 cake of yeast or 1 pkg. Fleishmann's dry yeast dissolved in 2 pints of warm water.
Add 2 tablespoons of sugar
Add 2 pints of flour
Mix in crock and let rise until very light and slightly aged, 24 to 48 hours, but do not let it get too sour and do not let the sponge chill.

Biscuits

Form a nest or hollow in pan of sifted flour. Pour approximately 2 cups of "starter" into the hollow; add 1/2 teaspoon salt; 1 tablespoon sugar; 2 heaping teaspoons baking powder sprinkled over sponge. Mix well to a soft firm dough. Turn out on a lightly floured board. Opinions differ among chuck wagon cooks about what to use to roll biscuits, some think a Four Roses bottle is best, while others use Three Feathers or Old Crow, as for myself, I pat the dough to a thickness of 1/2 inch. Cut the biscuits with a small cutter (10 cent Bak. Powdr. can is good) and put into well greased pans. Tin plates give excellent results. Grease tops of biscuits generously.

Sour Dough Biscuits, like cowboys, need a rest, so at this point set them in a warm place to rise from 3 to 5 minutes before baking. Bake in a very hot oven, 500 degrees, until nicely browned, 10 or 12 minutes.

The closer the biscuits are crowded into the pan for baking the higher they will rise. The heat for baking Sour Dough Biscuits is a very important factor. Preheat the oven so that you are sure of a steady high temperature at the time the biscuits are put into the oven.

If you have some dough left after making Sour Dough Biscuits, do not throw it away, but return it to the crock with the "starter", add a cup of warm water and the amount of flour to mix to consistency of first "starter." If a larger amount of "starter" is desired, add more water and flour. Set aside until biscuit time again. You never have to add yeast after the first time.

For best results your "starter" should be used daily, If not used often it will get sour and die, then you will have to make a new starter. In case it gets a little sour by not using it for two or three days, especially in warm weather, it will still give good results by adding 1/4 to 1/2 teaspoon of soda dissolved in a little warm water along with the baking powder. Do not be discouraged if your first Sour Dough Biscuits are not a howling success as the "starter" improves with age. Some cooks are known to have kept the same "starter" going for years.

Idaho Cowboy Beans

2 cups pinto beans
2 teaspoons salt
1 large onion, coarsely chopped
2 large cloves garlic, chopped
1 whole bay leaf
1 (No. 2 can) whole tomatoes
1/2 cup green bell pepper, chopped
1/4 teaspoon oregano
2 tablespoons brown sugar
1 teaspoon dry mustard
ham hock or boiling meat

Cook all ingredients together except tomatoes, then add tomatoes after 1 1/2 hours cooking time. Finish cooking slowly while covered. Remove bay leaf after beans are tender and ready to serve.

Cowboy Breakfast Pie

1 pound regular bulk sausage
1 pound hot bulk sausage
1 medium onion, finely chopped
4 or 5 stalks celery, finely chopped
1 (4.5 ounce) can mild diced green Chile peppers
8 slices bread, toasted, or 3 cups flavored croutons
1 can cream of mushroom soup
4 eggs
2 1/2 cups milk
10 ounces Cheddar, mozzarella or jack cheese

In a large skillet, cook both sausages together until done. Drain off grease. Chop onions and celery fairly fine and add to fried sausage. Fry onions and celery with sausage until onions and celery are about half cooked. Pour sausage, onions, and celery into a large pan or bowl. Add croutons, eggs, peppers, mushroom soup, and milk. Add 1 cup cheese and mix well.

Spoon 1/2 mixture into a buttered 9 x 13-inch dish. Spread 1/2 remaining cheese lightly over layer. Spread remaining mixture and cover with remaining cheese. Bake at 350 degrees F for 35 minutes. Uncover and bake at 300 degrees F for another 30 to 35 minutes. Remove from oven when cheese starts to darken around edges. Best to let cool before serving so it can set up some. Serve with picante sauce.

Snowman ice cream

Ingredients

- 1 cup milk
- 1 beaten egg
- 1/2 cup sugar
- Sprinkle of salt
- 1 teaspoon vanilla or other flavoring
- Clean snow

Instructions

Blend ingredients above really well and add clean, fresh snow, and mix until icy cold.

The cowboy who drank
three mugs of beer

A cowboy at a bar in Great Falls, MT. orders three mugs of beer and sits in the back room, drinking a sip out of each one in turn. When he finishes them, he comes back to the bar and orders three more. The bartender tells him, "You know, a mug goes flat after I draw it. It would taste better if you bought one at a time."

The cowboy replies, "I know. But that's OK. I have two brothers. One is in Billings, the other in Helena. I'm in Great Falls. When we left home, we promised that we'd drink this way to remember the days we drank together. I drink one for each of my brothers and one for myself."

The bartender tells him it is a nice custom. The cowboy becomes a regular, and always orders three mugs and drinks them in turn. One day he comes in and orders two mugs. All the regulars take notice and fall silent. When he comes back to the bar for the second round, the bartender says, "We don't want to intrude on your grief, but we wanted to offer our condolences on your loss."

The cowboy looks quite puzzled for a moment, then a light dawns and he laughs. "Oh, no, everybody's just fine," he explains. "It's just that my wife and I joined the Mormon Church and I had to quit drinking. Hasn't affected my brothers though."

Chapter 7

Fenced In by Barbed Wire

> Animals often offered the only companionship for long periods in the cowboy's life and, through intimate contact, he came to see their "human side" and to understand himself better as a "human animal."
>
> (*The Humor of the American Cowboy*)

Development of barbed wire had as much as anything to do with the demise of the cowboy. With barbed wire to keep the cattle on their own range, there was little need for the cowboy other than to mend fences.

Two factions tried to get the patent rights for barbed wire, and it was only after a furious legal battle that Joseph Glidden was considered the "Father of Barbed Wire."

Even that is historically incorrect, however, as in 1863, a Michael Kelly developed a type of fence with points affixed to twisted strands of wire. Kelly, however, failed to patent his invention.

It wasn't until ten years later that Joseph Glidden, Jacob Haish and Isaac Ellwood visited the DeKalb County Fair in Illinois. There they viewed an exhibit for a "wooden strip with metallic points" created by a farmer named Henry Rose. Rose's device was nothing more than a strip of wood armed with nail-like spikes. When attached to a wire fence, it would supposedly deter animals.

Glidden, Haish and Ellwood believed they could improve on Rose's crude invention and within two years each of the men had obtained his own patent. Joseph Glidden made his first barbed wire in the kitchen of his farmhouse, using a coffee mill to twist the barbs into shape.

He then utilized a grindstone to twist two strands of wire together after placing the handmade barbs on one strand of the wire. After making several hundred feet of wire in this manner, he fenced his wife's vegetable garden to keep out stray animals.

Meanwhile, Isaac Ellwood, a hardware merchant, had been unsuccessful in perfecting his own version of barbed wire. But when Joseph Glidden was awarded a patent on November 24, 1874 for his creation known as "The Winner," he and Ellwood formed a partnership to establish The Barb Fence Company.

Jacob Haish, the third man in the trio, had patented his own wire by this time but had not made a serious attempt to promote and sell it. Haish did want the credit for barbed wire, and didn't like the idea of Glidden and Ellwood forming a partnership. He was determined to bring them down.

When Haish learned that Glidden had applied for a patent in late 1873, but was denied, Haish filed a patent for his own

Glidden barbed wire design

creation, the "S-Barb" in July of 1874. A few days later he filed interference papers against Glidden and an intense legal dispute ensued.

Even though Haish was the first to be awarded a patent, Glidden won the dispute because he had filed his patent before Haish. Unwilling to admit defeat, Haish claimed the title of "the inventor of barbed wire." Nevertheless, it was Joseph Glidden who became known as the "Father of Barbed Wire."

Before barbed wire could achieve widespread use throughout the West, it had to be accepted by ranchers and farmers. Sensing that Texas would be the largest single market for the fencing product, Ellwood sent the team of Henry Sanborn and J.P. Warner to Houston to promote and sell barbed wire.

They found Texas seething with controversy between the free grassers, who wanted to maintain the open range, and the nesters, who advocated fields protected by fences. Even those who were in favor of fencing scoffed at the idea that a light-weight barbed wire fence could restrain the wild Texas Longhorn cattle.

There was also concern that the sharp barbs would inflict wounds on cattle. If the cuts became infected, the cattle could become diseased and die. Because of these controversies, Sanborn and Warner failed to sell much barbed wire.

Ellwood then hired 21-year-old salesman John W. Gates to go to Texas. Gates first obtained permission to build a barbed wire corral in San Antonio's Military Plaza. He announced that he would demonstrate that his barbed wire fence could contain even the wildest Texas Longhorns, and, to prove his point, offered to take all bets on the outcome.

Gates' daring proposal aroused the interest of cattlemen. When the fenced enclosure was complete, wild longhorn bulls were driven into the corral. The animals, aroused by the taunts of the onlookers, repeatedly charged the barbed wire. The fences held and Gates soon began to sell barbed wire to the cattlemen by the railcar load.

The first really big customers for barbed wire, however, were the railroads. As the lines moved west across the prairies, cattlemen and farmers were alarmed by the loss of their livestock on the unfenced tracks. In 1876, for example, the Missouri, Kansas & Texas Railroad reported that 1,948 animals had been killed in the three states where it operated, costing the railroads about $25,000.

In the American southwest barbed-wire fencing led to disputes known as the range wars between free-range ranchers and farmers. These were similar to the disputes, which resulted from "enclosure law" in England in the early 18th century.

These disputes were decisively settled in favor of the farmers, and heavy penalties were instituted for cutting the wire in a barbed-wire fence.

The so-called sheep wars, conflicts between cattlemen and sheepmen over grazing rights, took place between the early 1870s and 1900. Fundamental differences between sheep and cattle meant that they required different amounts of water, different types of food, and different manners of herding.

Cattlemen felt they had established priority in most areas of Texas by being there first, and they resented encroachment of the sheepman on their ranges. The cattlemen were the more aggressive of the two factions, and they used various method of intimidation against the sheepmen.

Both the cattlemen and the settled sheepmen attacked the nomadic sheepmen or "drifters", accusing them of twisting or rolling fences to allow their flocks to pass. The drifters were resented also because their flocks were too often infected with scab disease.

In 1875, cowboys and sheepmen clashed on the Charles Goodnight range and in the Texas-New Mexico boundary area. Several West Texas counties were scenes for the range wars. An 1881 law finally provided appointment of sheep inspectors and the quarantining of diseased sheep. This act drove the drifters under cover. Laws forbidding sheepmen to herd sheep on the open range were ineffective because no representatives of the General Land Office were located in West Texas.

Texas legislators, then, in 1883, enacted a law requiring a certificate of inspection to show that sheep were free of scab before they could be moved across a county line. This soon put a stop to nomadic sheepherders from out of state using Texas lands.

Because of the rush for the leasing of public lands, many sheepmen could not secure adjoining pastures. Consequently, they were forced to drive their flocks across the land of other stockmen. A code evolved that required the sheepherder to drive his flocks at least five miles a day on level terrain, or at least three miles a day in rougher country.

When a case came to court, the cowman was usually declared the winner. After the passage of the law of 1884, which made fence-cutting a felony, both the cattlemen and sheepmen restricted their livestock to their own ranges. This brought an end to the sheep wars.

In Kansas, lawmakers wrote legally binding definitions of proper fencing. When cropland adjoined land used for grazing, Kansas placed the burden on the landowner to fence out cattle lawfully at large.

This was based on free range grazing laws, which permitted cattle to graze unrestrained. While the farmer was responsible for constructing the fence, he was also afforded many advantages for doing so.

If an animal breached a fence and trespassed upon cultivated land, the animal's owner was held responsible for any damage.

The landowner could retain possession of the animal until he was properly compensated.

Railroads were required to construct a legally defined fence along the right of way wherever tracks crossed legally fenced private land. Railroads did not receive the same benefits granted to landowners, however. They were exempted from rights of recourse when livestock trespassed upon their right of way.

Another problem arose when neighboring farmers and ranchers decided to "borrow" wire from railroad fences for their own use. With the enormous amount of barbed wire fencing material being legitimately sold, it was virtually impossible to find the thief and recover the stolen wire.

This led to wire manufacturers designing unique variations in barbed wire design exclusively for use by the railroads. These designs consisted of one or more square strands of wire woven among one or more traditional round lines.

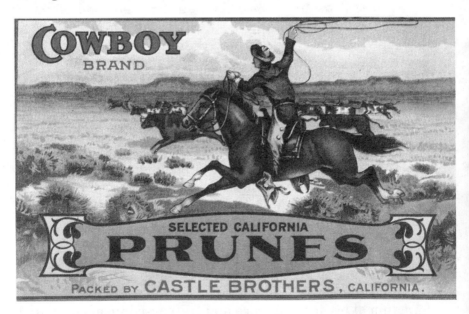

Cowboys ate a lot of dried fruit while on the trail or riding the range. A California prune company took notice of the fact and used the cowboy's image to market its fruit. (Prints and Photographs Division, Library of Congress)

Chapter 8

The Horses They Rode

> Morally, as a class, cowboys are foulmouthed, blasphemous, drunken, lecherous, and utterly corrupt. Usually harmless on the plains, when sober, they are dreaded in towns, for then liquor has an ascendancy over them
> (Cheyenne Daily Leader)

The Spanish brought several types of horses to the Americas when Spain was colonizing Mexico and Texas Territory. In their small boats, they brought strains of early Andalusians, Ginetes, Sorraias, and perhaps even Garrano type horses.

Horse thieves were in evidence even during Columbus' day. The voyager complained to King Ferdinand that on his second voyage, he had paid for good horses. While he was away from the docks, however, peasant horses had been loaded onto his ships.

This actually may have been fortuitous, for the smaller hardy peasant stock probably had a higher survival rate during the voyages than the bigger and higher bred Andalusians.

The Spaniards brought horses to North America by four different routes—California, New Mexico, Texas and Florida. In a very short time the Indian tribes had acquired horses, usually by raids, and became expert horsemen.

History notes that Lewis and Clark traded for horses with the Snake Indians when his party crossed the Rocky Mountains shortly after 1800. These horses were descended from the Spanish stock brought over by Columbus.

The big cow outfits used scores of horses. Each rider was assigned five or six mounts for his own string. (Library of Congress)

In the 17th century, herds of horses were running wild from Mexico to the Canadian border. The Spanish mustang is descended from the horses turned loose by the Conquistadors when they no longer needed them.

One descendent of these horses, the *mustang,* migrated through Mexico to the United States. It was these Spanish horses that gathered the longhorns and drove them to the northern markets from the Texas plains.

In his memoirs, Colonel Richard I. Dodge wrote about a race between three Thoroughbred racehorses and a Comanche horse that took place before the Civil War. Officers at Fort Chadbourne, north of San Angelo, Texas owned the Thoroughbreds.

It was the practice of the officers to race their least fast horses first and then work up to the fastest horse running last when the bets were highest. A Comanche whose tribe was camped near the Fort challenged them. The Comanche horse was a miserable-appearing, sheepish-looking animal.

A Bureau of Land Management wrangler drives wild mustangs to a collection chute. (BLM photo)

When the race was run, the Indian pony easily won, causing great surprise to the army officers. The bets were doubled, and in less than an hour the same Comanche horse faced the second fastest of the racehorses.

The face markings of a horse: Top left, bald-faced; center, star; right top, stripe; lower left, snip; bottom center, star; bottom right, stripe.

Again, the Indian pony was victorious. Determined to recoup their money, the officers brought out their champion, a mare with famed Lexington breeding that regularly beat the two horses that had just lost to the Indian pony in a fourteen hundred yard dash

When the final race began, the Comanche rider gave a whoop and threw away the whip he had used to encourage his mount in the previous races. The Indian immediately took the lead.

Fifty yards from the finish line, The Comanche swung his leg around and rode backward, making faces at the rider of the Thoroughbred as his own Indian pony flashed across the finish line. Too late, the army officers learned that this little Indian pony had won six hundred horses for his tribe in a bet with the Kickapoo Indians.

Colonel Dodge, who told the above story, once offered Pony Express rider forty dollars for his mount. The rider looked surprised and told him the price for the horse was six hundred dollars, a very high price for the time.

Dodge later learned that the pony carried mail between El Paso and Chihuahua, about three hundred miles each way. The rider once made the trip on three consecutive nights and earned one hundred dollars per trip.

The Pony Express rider had been making the trip weekly for six months, and this had not diminished the fire or flesh of the little Spanish horse.

It is little wonder that the mustang became the favorite horse of the trail cowboy.

Recipe for Indian Whiskey
As told by Teddy Blue Abbott

"Indian Whiskey was invented by the Missouri River traders in the early days. You take one barrel of Missouri River water and two gallons of alcohol.

Then you add two ounces of strychnine to make them crazy—because strychnine is the greatest stimulant in the world—and three plugs of tobacco to make them sick—because an Indian wouldn't figure it was whiskey unless it made him sick—and five bars of soap to give it a head, and half a pound of red pepper, and then you put in some sagebrush and boil it until it's brown.

Strain this into a barrel and you've got your Indian Whiskey. One bottle calls for one buffalo robe, and when the Indian got drunk, it was two robes. And that's how some of the traders made their fortune.

Chapter 9

The Black Cowboys

> Of the estimated 35,000 cowboys that worked the ranches and rode the trails, between five and nine thousand was said to have been black. They participated in almost all of the trail drives northward and were assigned to every job except that of trail boss.

Black cowboys were seldom recognized for their role in western history. Historians in New Spain (Mexico) recognized the black cowboy, but it was as a lesser person than his white *compadres*.

New Spain in 1574 revised the Mesta (a forerunner of stock breeders' associations). This revision forbade mestizos, Indians, mulattoes, and Negro vaqueros to own horses. Ranchers had to provide the mounts for these riders they employed.

The wages of these early cowboys' also had to be paid with money, not in colts or other livestock. The revisions were an attempt to reduce cattle theft. No one was authorized to purchase livestock except from the ranch owner or his representative, except in a public place.

Violation of the code resulted in various forms of punishment which also had to do with the ethnic character of the violator. If a Spaniard broke the law, he was fined fifty pesos, or, if he could not pay the fine, given fifty lashes. For a second offense, the Spaniard was banished for a distance of 20 leagues (about 50 miles) from the district.

If the offender was a Negro, mulatto, mestizo, or Indian, the punishment was more severe. The first offense was 100 lashes.

These cowboys posing for a picture in Denver reflect the mix of races that rode the cattle trails of the west. (*Reprinted from The Wild West*)

The penalty was doubled for a second offense, plus an added sanction—cutting off the offender's ears. Kenneth Wiggins Porter in his book, *Negro on the American Frontier*, placed the number of Negroes at one-fourth of those on the trail during the generation following the Civil War.

Porter writes that eight or nine thousand black cowboys made up one-quarter of the total number of trail cowboys that were herding cattle to northern markets. Without their help, he said, "The cattle industry would have been seriously handicapped."

Being a black cowboy provided a chance for more opportunities and more dignity than in many other forms of employment for the Negro. As cowboys, their ability and courage won respect from their fellow cowboys.

Porter writes, "They were often paid the same wages as white cowboys, and in the case of certain horsebreakers, ropers, and cooks, occupied positions of considerable prestige. In a region and period characterized by violence, their lives were probably safer than they would have been in the southern cotton regions where between 1,500 and 1,600 Negroes were lynched in the two decades after 1882."

This doesn't mean the cow country was a utopia for Negroes, Porter stressed, but it did demonstrate that under some circumstances and for at least brief periods white and black in significant numbers could live and work together."

The history of black cowboys began long before the establishment of large ranches with cattle grazing in the nineteenth century, according to Bennie J. McRae, Jr.

In Gambia and some other African countries, there were large herds of cattle tended by natives that possessed many of the skills of present day cowboys. They were not called cowboys, but simply herders.

This particular group of blacks attracted the attention of slave traders and slave buyers in the southern states. When they were purchased prior to the Civil War, the slaves were used to hunt and work cattle in the tall grass, pine groves and marshes of South Carolina and other sections of the lower south. They worked in gangs on what was then called cattle plantations."

Few of these cattle tenders were ever mounted, and most used dogs, bullwhips, and salt to manage the cattle.

The northern states of Mexico became a favorite target of runaway slaves. The principal occupation in these areas was cattle and sheep ranching, and the ex-slaves swapped skills with the vaqueros. The blacks taught the vaqueros their skills in tending cattle, and the vaqueros taught the ex-slaves the skills of horseback riding and roping.

In fact, some historians contend that the very origin of the word "cowboy" was black. Children of former slaves used to be "cowhands" on ranches, and were always called "boy", as in, "Hey boy, go feed the cows." Eventually, the two words were put together for "cowboy."

Fifteen-year-old Nate Love was born a slave.
(Reprinted from *The Wild West*)

Right after the Civil War, thousands of blacks went to work on the ranches throughout south and west Texas.

One such black cowboy was Nate Love, born as a slave in Tennessee. He found a Texas outfit that had just delivered its herd and was preparing to return to Texas. Nate noticed there were several black cowboys in the outfit.

He shared breakfast with the crew and then asked the trail boss for a job. The boss told Nate that he would hire him if could break a horse named "Good Eye", the wildest horse in the outfit. Another black cowboy gave Nate some pointers and Nate rode the horse, the toughest horse he ever rode, he said later.

The first time Nate saw hostile Indians, he admitted he was too scared to run. He later bought a forty-five and practiced constantly, eventually becoming the best shot of all his friends.

Nate proved his prowess after joining a trail drive that delivered three thousand head of steers to Deadwood City in Dakota Territory. The trail drive arrived on July 3 and the town was getting ready to celebrate the Fourth of July.

Townsmen had organized a contest. Two hundred dollars would go to the cowboy that could rope, throw, tie bridles (make a halter), and saddle a mustang in the fastest time. Half of the men entering the contest were black.

The wildest horses were chosen for the event. Nate roped, threw, tied bridles, saddled, and mounted his mustang in exactly nine minutes. His nearest competitor took twelve minutes and thirty seconds.

In the rifle and pistol events he proved superior, too. Shooting at both 100 and 250 yards, Nate Love placed all of his rifle shots in the bull's eye and 10 of 12 of his pistol shots in the bull's eye.

Along with the money, Deadwood City bestowed on Nate Love the title of "Deadwood Dick."

Another black that made a name as a cowboy was Bose Ikard. He too, like Nate Love, was born a slave in Tennessee. His owner, Dr. Milton L. Ikard, took him to Texas to work on a cattle ranch.

He worked for Dr. Ikard even after his emancipation, but in 1866, he hired out to Charles Goodnight, one of the great trail drivers of the west, and one of the men that established the "Goodnight-Loving Cattle Trail."

Goodnight had nothing but praise for Ikard. "Bose surpassed any man I had in endurance and stamina. There was a dignity, a cleanliness and reliability about him that was wonderful. His behavior was very good in a fight and he was probably the most devoted man to me that I ever knew. I have trusted him farther than any man. He was my banker, my detective, and everything else in Colorado, New Mexico and the other wild parts of the country. The nearest and only bank was in Denver, and when we carried money, I gave it to Bose, for a thief would never think of robbing him."

Ikard married and settled in Weatherford Texas after his work in the cattle drives ended. He died at age eighty-five in 1929. Charles Goodnight had a granite marker erected at his grave.

Just as other cowboys, black riders could be wild and reckless. Such was the case of "Bronco Sam" whose real name has sort of slipped through the history book cracks.

Sam felt he could ride any horse in the world. At a big rodeo in Cheyenne, the other cowboys in his trail crew decided it would be fun to rope the biggest longhorn in the herd, saddle it up, and have Sam ride through town.

When saddled, with Sam on top, the longhorn turned into a tornado. It was frightened and wild-eyed, and when it saw its image in the window of a clothing store, it pawed the ground and charged right through the window.

Sales clerks dove for protection while the steer plunged through the clothing racks. Then, it charged back out through the window it had come in through.

Sam was still in the saddle as the steer raced down the street with pants, coats and underwear decorating its horns. As the cowboys closed in to drive the steer back to the herd, Sam shouted, "I brought out a suit of clothes for everybody in the crew."

Back at the herd, Sam got off the steer and saddled his horse to return to town with his rowdy partners. When the storekeeper spotted the crew, he gave them a deservedly cold reception.

Sam, however, was unruffled and cool. He smiled, and apologized to the retailer, and asked what the damages were. When the shopkeeper tallied up a bill, it came to three hundred and fifty dollars. Not batting an eye, Sam peeled off the amount and handed it over. He then went to work as a cowboy on a ranch near Cheyenne.

There were numerous other black cowboys that made the drives out of Texas to the northern markets.

There were also a lot of black cowboys that made a place as professional rodeo cowboys.

Black Cowboy Bill Pickett
He invented the Bulldogging
event in the sport of rodeo.
(National Geographic)

One of the more famous was William (Bill) Pickett, who had both black and Indian blood. From 1905 to 1931, the Miller Brothers 101 Ranch Wild West Show was one of the shows that traveled the country much like William F. "Buffalo Bill" Cody's show did in 1883.

One event the show introduced was that of bulldogging or steer wrestling, invented by black cowboy Bill Pickett.

Riding his horse "Spradley", Bill pull alongside a steer, dropped down and grasped the steer's head and horns while bringing the animal to a stop by digging his heels into the dirt. To gain control of the steer, Bill would bite the upper lip of the steer. He had seen cowdogs of the Bulldog breed bite the lips of cattle to subdue them. That's how Pickett's technique got the name "bulldogging." Bill Pickett is in the Cowboy Hall of Fame.

At age 62, Bill Pickett was kicked in the head by a horse and died eleven days later of a skull fracture. He was buried at

White Eagle Monument, in Marland, Oklahoma. Pickett was a good friend of Will Rogers who announced the cowboy's death on his national radio show.

Another black cowboy that cut a stride in the rodeo game was Jesse Stahhl, a bronc rider. In the early 1900s, Jesse competed in an Oregon rodeo. Virtually all hands agreed it was an exceptional ride and worthy of first place.

The judges, however, awarded him second place. It was clear to the cowboys that a case of skin color was factored into the decision of the judges.

To protest the judges' decision, Jesse rode his next bronc facing backwards, carrying a suitcase in his hand.

Few black cowboys ever held the position of range boss. One that did was Addison Jones, who rode the Goodnight-Loving Trail in New Mexico.

"Add" was the range boss of the LFD outfit and usually headed a crew of south Texas black cowboys. Cowboys from Tozah, Texas to Las Vegas and New Mexico knew "Add" and many of them, at different times, worked on roundups with him.

Mr. Add was said to be a virtual dictionary on earmarks and brands. During one roundup, however, the number of brands on one critter puzzled him. "She's got O Block an Lightnin' Rod, Nine Forty-Six an' A Bar Eleven, Rafter Cross an' de double prod, Terrapin an' Ninety-Seven. Since none of the cowpunchers attending the roundup claimed the animal, Add said, "I'll just add my own brand, cause one more brand or less won't do no harm."

Another interesting tale is that of Matt Hooks, known to all his friends as "Bones". Bones established a reputation as a master horse breaker.

He then took a job as a Pullman porter on the Santa Fe Railroad out of Amarillo. When he heard rumors of an "unbreakable" horse at Pampa, a town east of Amarillo, it stirred his attention. Every time the train stopped at Pampa, Bones would hear more stories of how the best riders in the west had paid their entry fees in a rodeo only to be defeated by that horse.

The purse rose to $250, but still nobody could break the animal. One day, some cattlemen boarded the train and were full of talk about the outlaw horse. One of them was a man for whom Bones had previously worked. Bones told him he would like to break that wild bronco.

The rancher said, "We think a lot of you Bones, but we don't want to see a good porter get hurt."

"Just get two hundred fifty dollars and have the horse down at the train in Pampa and I'll ride it while the train is in the station. If I don't you can give my money to the Sunday school and hang me."

A date was set. At the appointed time, Bones arrived at the train in Amarillo wearing a Stetson hat and cowboy boots. The conductor refused to let him board, demanding an explanation of how Bones was dressed.

Bones told him he was going to ride the outlaw horse.

"What'll happen if you break a leg?" the conductor asked. "What'll the Santa Fe officials say if I let my porter ride a bronc while he's on duty?"

They agreed to talk to the engineer.

"How long will it take, Bones?" asked the engineer.

"Five minutes," Bones replied.

"Well, we can make that time up, so I'm willing to let him try," said the engineer.

News had spread about the event and numerous bets were made. All the passengers unloaded to see the contest. Bone's rancher friend was unable to attend, but wired ahead the instructions and the two hundred and fifty dollar purse.

The purse was handed to the nervous conductor who still looked unhappy about the whole affair.

The horse was brought forward, blindfolded, saddled and tightly held. With one swift motion, Bones snatched the blindfold from the animal's head and leaped into the saddle. In less than the five minutes allowed, the black rider rode the horse until it stopped pitching. He then quietly dismounted.

The train whistle blew its signal and the passengers reloaded. Before Bones headed back to the Pullman car, he stopped briefly at the telegraph window in the Pampa station and sent a message to his rancher friend. "Outlaw rode. Got money. Gone east. Bones."

Chapter 10

Cattle Brands

> Fugitives, galley slaves, gypsies, vagabonds, brawlers and the clergy have been marked with "symbols of shame" brands down through history. Brands have been used as marks of identification at some time in all countries and civilizations.

The branding of cattle to establish ownership dates to the early Egyptian dynasties of 3,000 B.C. One brief history of branding says both cattle and humans were branded some 4,000 years ago.

Cattle raising and branding began with the importation of Spanish Criollo cattle by Columbus on his second voyage to the New World in 1493.

Some historians claim Hernando Cortez introduced both cattle and the art of branding to the new world in 1520.

The *Three Crosses* brand of Hernando Cortes, signifying the Holy Trinity, was the first brand recorded in North America. Scenes of branded cattle and the process of branding have been uncovered on the walls of ancient Egyptian tombs.

In Spanish Texas, brands and earmarks were registered in brand books maintained by the *ayuntamientos*, or municipal councils. After 1878, the provincial government in San Antonio maintains an official brand book for all of Spanish Texas.

Nothing equaled the branding iron in determining the matters of ownership on the open range. Many cattlemen named their ranches after their brand and were as proud of the symbol as knights of old were of their crests.

During roundup, various ranchers joined together to sort, brand and earmark their calves. (Prints and Photographs Division, Library of Congress)

Spanish brands were more complicated and rich in design than the brands adopted by American cattlemen. American ranchers wanted brands that were simple in design, easy to remember, and easily made.

There were two types of branding iron, the "stamp iron" which included the full brand, and the so-called "running iron" which had a hooked tip that could be used to change or make any brand.

Brands are more than a means of identifying cattle. Burned into the hide of a cow, a brand identifies the animal's owner—a vital necessity in open range where several different ranches may run their cattle together.

But the brand does more. It has come to stand for the outfit itself, the ranch, its owners, its workers, and its traditions.

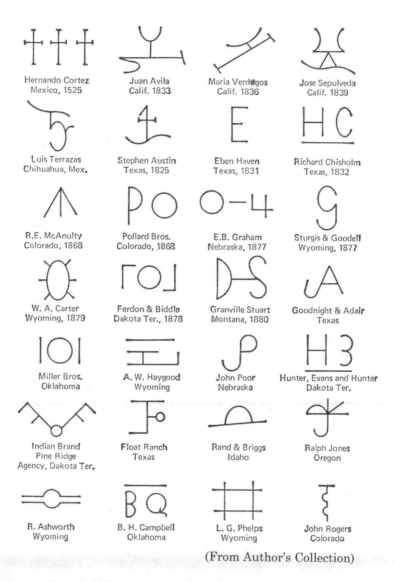

Hernando Cortez Mexico, 1525	Juan Avila Calif. 1833	Maria Verdugos Calif. 1836	Jose Sepulveda Calif. 1839
Luis Terrazas Chihuahua, Mex.	Stephen Austin Texas, 1825	Eben Haven Texas, 1831	Richard Chisholm Texas, 1832
R.E. McAnulty Colorado, 1868	Pollard Bros. Colorado, 1868	E.B. Graham Nebraska, 1877	Sturgis & Goodell Wyoming, 1877
W. A. Carter Wyoming, 1879	Ferdon & Biddle Dakota Ter., 1878	Granville Stuart Montana, 1880	Goodnight & Adair Texas
Miller Bros. Oklahoma	A. W. Haygood Wyoming	John Poor Nebraska	Hunter, Evans and Hunter Dakota Ter.
Indian Brand Pine Ridge Agency, Dakota Ter.	Float Ranch Texas	Rand & Briggs Idaho	Ralph Jones Oregon
R. Ashworth Wyoming	B. H. Campbell Oklahoma	L. G. Phelps Wyoming	John Rogers Colorado

(From Author's Collection)

Because there were few skilled iron workmen among the early Americans, and proper equipment was lacking, some

81

ranchers branded only with a "running iron" or "ring". Use of these tools meant the man placing the brand was essentially drawing the design onto the animals hide.

The running iron was made from a piece of iron 20 to 30 inches long and about one-fourth inch in diameter. One end was bent to form a U, while the other end was offset to use as a handle.

While the original intent of the running iron and the iron ring were honorable, crafty cattle rustlers used the running iron and the ring to change legitimate brands. The most famous brand change involved the altering of the X I T brand into a Star with a cross inside.

The running iron is credited for the large number of single letters and numbers recorded in the early days. They were simply easier to make than was a complicated brand. A simple brand design is preferable because it is easier to read and also causes less stress to the animal.

A suspected cattle rustler caught carrying a running iron might find himself in deep trouble. A vigilante group would mostly likely string the suspect up immediately.

A good hot brand is recognizable because it destroys hair follicles located under several layers of skin and leaves permanent scar on the hide of the animal. The secret to successful hot branding is destroying the hair follicles without burning through the hide itself.

Iron temperature is an important element in branding. If the iron looks black, it is too cold; if it glows red, it is too hot. An iron that is the color of gray ashes is the proper temperature and will produce a good brand.

An animal that is branded wet will usually not have a clear brand, as moisture transfers the heat over a larger area. This will result in an unreadable blotched brand.

Cattle brands have been used as marks of identification at some time in all countries and civilizations. Until modern times, to prevent theft, livestock being driven across county were required to be "road branded". The brands were painted on with

82

pine tar or paint in early history. Later on, when the trail herds were driven north to market, hot iron brands were used.

An unbranded animal is called a "slick" and virtually impossible to identify. No other identification method is as accurate or easily visible as branding.

Brand language is highly readable to stockmen but may be mumbo-jumbo to a person unacquainted with the process. In brand language, letters may be "crazy, swinging, rocking, running, tumbling, dragging, or flying among others. Brands may include a slash, a circle, a cross, square or box, or combinations of each of them.

Before the widespread use of fencing to contain cattle on designated ranges, brands and earmarks were used to identify the cattle. Brands are read much like books, from top to bottom and left to right.

Chapter 11

The Hanging Windmill

> The ingenious ranch owner didn't need an
> army, he didn't even need a ranch. What he
> needed was a brand, a spot to put a chuck
> wagon on, a large herd of cattle and a group
> of eight or nine cowhands who worked for
> love, not money.

It turned out to be a bad day when Manuel Barela entered the Flores Saloon in Las Vegas, New Mexico June 4, 1879.

All that Barela wanted was a pint of wine. He was in charge of a wagon train owned by his brother, Mariano Barela, and had been whooping it up while camped outside Las Vegas for the past several days.

Barela had obviously been imbibing before entering the saloon. He bet the bartender that he could shoot the buttons off the vest of one of the two men talking just outside the saloon door. He drew his six-shooter and fired. The bullet struck one of the men in the face, inflicting a severe but not fatal wound.

When the man's seventy-year-old companion, Begnigno Romero, confronted Barela, asking him why he shot his friend, Barela answered by firing two shots into Romero's body, killing him instantly.

Las Vegas lawmen arrived on the scene and arrested Barela while angry townsmen wanted to lynch him on the spot. The officers got Barela safely to jail and locked him away.

The *Las Vegas Gazette* ran the following article:

> *"The person killed was a hardworking old man.
> He had stopped before the saloon to talk of his work
> next day. He was an entire stranger to Barela, and*

85

neither he nor his companion had given him the slightest pretext for offense. The shooting was entirely without provocation, a devilish and crazy freak which should not go unpunished."

The *Hanging Windmill* at Las Vegas, New Mexico.
(Museum of New Mexico)

A heavy guard was placed on Barela to keep him from being lynched. The evening passed without sign of trouble.

About midnight, the silence was broken by the sound of gunshots on a nearby hill. Somebody called for the police, and all but a couple of the guards watching Barela scurried to the scene on the hilltop.

A large crowd of citizens then converged on the jail and overpowered the remaining guards. They forced the jailor to hand over the keys to Barela's cell, and, while there, decided to do double duty and took along another prisoner, Giovanni Dugi, who was also being held for murder.

The prisoners were marched to the center of the plaza where an odd-shaped wooden windmill stood. Wooden ladders led up to a platform and on to the top.

Barela was hanged in bright moonlight, and when he had expired, Dugi met the same fate. The *Gazette* reported:

> *"In half a minute after the hanging was accomplished, the plaza was perfectly clear of people and the town was as quiet as a graveyard."*

It wasn't long before the windmill claimed another victim. A young cowboy named Beckworth was twirling his pistol before an admiring audience. The gun went off and killed a man standing behind him.

Beckworth apologized, saying it was just an accident, and then resumed his pistol twirling again. Again the gun went off, this time killing a woman standing in the doorway of her house.

Officers quickly got Beckworth to jail. Even so, the next morning his body was found hanging from the windmill, along with a placard hanging from his neck, that read, *"This is no accident."*

Chapter 12

The Night Riders

These mysterious riders wore their white hoods to protect their identity. They rode their horses at night, burning crops, tearing out railroad ties, and harassing people.

They were called *Las Gorras Blancas* (The White Caps). The White Caps were vigilantes of San Miguel County, New Mexico, who fought furiously against any changes that came upon their land. The group was comprised mainly of native shepherds and farmers, who viewed the railroads as their enemy and not as a symbol of prosperity.

Anglos began buying land. They built fences to establish the fact that the land was indeed private property. This meant that neighbors could no longer graze their animals in these communal pastures.

Communities such as Sapello, one of several small towns in San Miguel County located along the Santa Fe Trail, couldn't cope with the rapid changes taking place. The coming of the railroad was causing them to lose their land, forcing them into unwanted career changes.

Before the railroad, Sapello's lifeline was the Santa Fe Trail. The Trail provided convenience in travel and in trade. People traveling through Sapello on their way to Mora County, Las Vegas and Santa Fe often stopped in Sapello and spent their money. Sapello was an important trading spot for travelers because of its location.

It is at this time that Las Gorras Blancas decided to restore the old ways by cutting fences and stopping the railroad.

This photo shows a reenactment of the Las Gorras Blancas nightriders.
(Brigham Young University)

These mysterious riders wore their white hoods to protect their identity. They rode their horses at night, burning crops, tearing out railroad ties, and harassing people.

Behind their masks, Las Gorras Blancas threatened with death anyone who associated with their hated target, the railroad. The nightriders made their mark by cutting fences and caused as much as twenty-seven thousand dollars worth of fence damage in 1880 alone.

They rode into the town of East Las Vegas, New Mexico just before midnight, March 11, 1890, two hundred riders strong. They paraded silently through the streets, crossed over the Gallinas River Bridge into West Las Vegas where they paused in front of the home of Sheriff Lorenzo Lopez.

They then moved on to the San Miguel County Courthouse and then to the jail, where they sat silently for a while before disappearing into the darkness.

This photo shows Las Vegas Plaza in the 1880s after the coming of the Santa Fe Railroad. (Museum of New Mexico)

Los Gorras Blancas had made such nocturnal visits before, but this time they scattered printed circulars explaining their fight against those who were appropriating and fencing tracts of common lands for their own use.

No one questioned that Los Gorras Blancas meant business. Appearing on horseback under cover of darkness, the White Caps tore down miles of wire fencing and fence posts, burned barns and haystacks and scattered livestock.

The cause of the turmoil was confusion over the status of the Las Vegas Community Land Grant. This grant was surveyed in 1860, with a resulting measure of 496,444.96 acres.

In 1835, the Mexican government set aside the lands surrounding Las Vegas, and within the grant boundaries, to be held in joint ownership by the original Las Vegas colonists and their heirs and successors. These lands were to be an undivided community and open for grazing, hunting and wood gathering.

U.S. officials, however, insisted that the common lands had become a part of the U.S. public domain, eligible for private settlement and development.

91

Anglos bought up and fenced tracts of land, moved livestock onto them, planted crops and diverted water from streams to irrigate. This put Hispanic farmers and ranchers who depended on these lands for their livelihood out in the cold.

Las Vegas people sympathized with the White Cap movement. Outside of Las Vegas the image of the vigilante group was not so good. They were pictured as anti-Anglo terrorists and outlaws who were giving New Mexico a bad name.

In their circulars, the White Caps explained their positions, which were printed by a number of New Mexico newspapers:

Our Platform

Not wishing to be misunderstood, we hereby make this our declaration:

Our purpose is to protect the rights and interests of the people in general, and especially those of the helpless classes.

We want the Las Vegas grant settled to the interest of all concerned, and this we hold is the entire community within the grant.

We want no "land grabbers" or obstructionists of any sort to interfere. We will watch them. We are not down on lawyers as a class, but the usual knavery and unfair treatment of the people must be stopped.

The position paper continued at length, and was signed by the White Caps, with the notation:

"1,500 Strong and Gaining Daily".

The White Caps continued with their raids and even extended them into adjoining Santa Fe and Mora counties.

Pablo Herrera, a former prison inmate, was elected to the New Mexico Territorial Legislature in the 1890 elections.

He sat quietly through several sessions of the Territorial Assembly in Santa Fe before deciding he had had enough. At the close of the legislative session, Herrera rose from his seat and delivered this brief address to his colleagues:

"Gentlemen, I have served several years time in the penitentiary but only sixty days in the Legislature, the present House of Representatives.

I have watched the proceedings here carefully.

I would like to say that the time I spent in the penitentiary was more enjoyable than the time I spent here.

There is more honesty in the halls of the territorial prison than in the halls of the Legislature.

I would prefer another term in prison than another election to the House."

His political career thus ended, a short time later Herrera was convicted of third degree murder in the stabbing death of Doroteo Sandoval in a West Las Vegas saloon.

A friendly jailor allowed Herrera to escape and a two hundred dollar reward was offered for his arrest. A sheriff's posse on a West Las Vegas street shot him to death on Christmas Eve, 1894.

By the time of Herrera's death, the White Cap raids in San Miguel County had ceased as there were no fences remaining on the common lands and no new ones were being built.

The land-grant matter was resolved in 1903 when the Town of Las Vegas was given ownership of the disputed lands and a board of trustees was established to administer them.

Chapter 13

Stampede

> *"You'd hear that low rumbling noise along the ground and the men on herd would not need to come in and tell you, you'd know. Then you'd jump on your horse and get them into a mill before they scattered to hell and gone."*

A stampede was the last thing a cowboy wanted to happen. It was probably the most dangerous occurrence that could happen to a cowboy on a trail drive.

Drawing from *The Longhorns* by J. Frank Dobie

The trail boss dreaded those nights when the air was full of tension, and even the slightest crack of thunder or bolt of lightening could set them off. Experienced cowboys knew there was a thousand things that could make the cattle jump and run.

It might be something as innocent as the yelp of a coyote, the whinny of a horse, or the flare of a match as a cowboy lighted a cigarette.

One story recalls that a stampede started when a hen from a settler's cabin flapped across the trail. The scattered cattle, after being rounded up, refused to pass that cabin again.

William Owens described one stampede in which he was involved. He worked for the Strayhorn Cattle Company in Arizona.

"We had gathered fifteen hundred critters for market. The cattle were bunched and ready to start drifting and we were intending to start the next morning at sun. About midnight a storm struck and lightening hit in the middle of the herd.

"As usual, the animals were fretful before the storm hit. They didn't bed down and were moving here and there. All hands were out trying to quiet the critters down.

"We were singing and whistling trying to give the critters comfort, but they were all set to run. They were just waiting for something that would start the running. The sky-fire was what furnished the excuse and they went off like a bunch of racehorses do when the gun is fired.

"At the jump we knew holding that herd was out of the question, so we just tried to keep those critters from scattering until they tuckered out a bit. It was dark and we couldn't see the herd or each other except when a flash of sky-fire lit up the country.

"We could hear the clashing of horns and could tell about where the herd was. We waddies kept each other posted on our location by firing several shots at a time. The first shot was to draw attention and other shots were given so the fire flash could be seen.

"It was ten miles to the Pareco River and we calculated on getting the critters under control before the river was reached, but we failed to do so. We reached the river and the critters were still going at a good rate of speed and about half the animals went into the water and four of the waddies did likewise before they realized where they were going.

"There was quicksand at the point where the bunch ran into the river. Immediately, there was plenty of scrambling and floundering men, cattle and hosses, in the dark and rain. No one could see enough to do anything and we just had to wait for daylight.

"The part of the herd that hit the water first blocked the other critters and stopped the run. We put the critters that were on land to milling. When daylight came, we found two waddies, Sandy Peters and Arizona Slim, drowned."

Two of the cowboys, Owens said, fished the cowboys that had drowned from the river. The rest of the crew set to work pulling bogged cows that were still alive from the stream. "We worked all day at pulling out bogged critters, but lost three hundred that drowned."

The saddened trail crew buried the two dead cowboys on the banks of the Pecco River.

"I was selected to do the preaching," Owens said, "and did the best I could. I requested the Lord, 'to take them in, because their hearts were pure as gold. While they were rough, tough and cussed, all their acts were done with good intentions. They were true to their fellow men, to their work and to every trust."

In 1872, Mark Withers was riding in the lead of a stampede on the Smoky River near Hays, Kansas. He saw by the flash of lightening that he was on the edge of a high cliff. His only recourse, he knew, was to spur on. He and his horse went over the cliff and landed in three or four feet of water. Neither the horse nor cowboy was injured.

Instead of going on across the river, Withers and his horse took refuge under the bluff. From this protected point, he saw by lightening flashes the steers pouring down. A large number of the cattle were killed or crippled.

Another cowboy, Frank Mitchell, with the **J A** outfit, was involved in a stampede related by J. Frank Dobie, western writer and former cowboy, who recognized that some cowboy tales grow with each telling. This was an especially tall tale.

"Talk about dark," Mitchell said. "It was darker'n the inside of a cow with her lights drilled out. The stompeders headed for a bluff that I didn't know existed and went on over like hell after a preacher. I was riding on their fetlocks when my night horse—and God, he was a good one—went with 'em.

"He didn't make a bobble goin' down, jest kept steady, his feet straight out. I don't know how long we was (sic) making the descent. I had time for several thoughts and could have rolled a cigarette maybe.

"I'm still a settin' in the saddle like a reg'lar hand when Flying Machine—that what I named him—hit on his all fours. Just hit and stood there like he wanted to rest a while. I sorter teched him with the spur, but he couldn't budge, it seemed.

"Derned if we didn't stay there till daylight, and then I see he's bogged up to his knees in solid rock. That little experience shore developed his eyesight, and after that he was a better night horse then ever."

Cowboy Teddy Blue Abbott rode in a stampede and described the harrowing experience in the book, "We Pointed Them North."

"If a storm came up and the cattle started running—you'd hear that low rumbling noise along the ground and the men on herd would not need to come in and tell you, you'd know—then you jump for your horse and get out there in the lead, trying to head them and get into a mill before they scattered to hell and gone."

It was riding at a dead run in the dark, Abbott said, with cut banks and prairie dog holes all around you, not knowing if the next jump would land you in a shallow grave.

"I helped to bury three of them in very shallow graves," he wrote. "The first one was after a run on the Blue River in '76. We camped close to the Blue River one night, near a big prairie dog town."

A 3-man outfit recruited Abbott to help drive five hundred steers to Lincoln Nebraska where they had been sold. Abbott was only fifteen years old at the time, but he knew the territory and the others didn't.

A storm came up and it was impossible for the four men to hold the stampeding cattle. When morning came, Abbott said one man was missing. "We went back to look for him, and we found him among the prairie dog holes, beside his horse."

He added, "The horse's ribs were scraped bare of hide and all the rest of horse and man was mashed into the ground as flat as a pancake. The only thing you could recognize was the handle of his six-shooter."

The thing that Abbott and the two other surviving cowboys couldn't get out of their minds, however, was the fact that they had milled the stampeding cattle around in circles all night right over where they had found the dead cowboy.

On one trail drive, a shred from a cowboy's pouch of chewing tobacco lodged in a steer's eye, setting off a raging charge that resulted in the death of two riders and the loss of 400 steers.

In a herd, there might be a half a dozen troublemakers that would jump for no good reason and start the other cattle to run. If the cook needed fresh beef, it was usually supplied by butchering one of these troublesome animals.

Range men dreaded a stampede not so much because of danger as the likelihood of losing cattle and the time entailed in getting the scattered her back together.

Cattle do not trail in a group. They string out in a long line. The cattle herd had its leaders. Several natural leaders usually take their places in front, while the others form an irregular line behind them. A herd of one thousand might stretch out for one to two miles on the trail.

The drovers worked in pairs, one on either side of the herd. The best cowboys were the "pointers," and worked near the head of the line. The other cowboys worked the flank and swing positions farther back. The least experienced were the men riding drag, bringing up the rear.

To stop a stampede, the drovers nearest the head of the herd would get in front of the leaders and turn them to the right, causing them to mill or move in a circle. The rest of the herd would be forced to follow the leaders into the milling circle.

The riders kept closing in on the herd, squeezing them into a tighter and tighter circle until the entire herd was moving slowly, going around and around. It was a big relief to stop a stampede.

Chapter 14

The Winter of 1886-87

> *"I'll tell you what kind of a climate it is,"* he responded. *"You want a buffalo overcoat, a linen duster and a slicker with you all the time."*

The harsh winter ended the era of the cattle business on the open range. Old timers recall the winter of 1886-87 as the time that crippled the cattle business.

To make the situation worse was the fact that the summer of 1886 was a dry, parching period when both the grass and the water holes dried up. Wild fires plagued the state. What little water there was in the creeks was so alkaline that cattle couldn't drink it.

It was "hell-on-earth" for the cattlemen during that dry summer, but they would find they hadn't seen hell at all until the winter of 1886 came. Temperatures dropped to seventy degrees below zero.

Joseph Kinsey Howard, in his book, *Montana High, Wide and Handsome*, wrote: "That fall wild game moved early from its favored shelters in the Missouri Badlands and hurried south and west. Birds which customarily remained all winter fled to warmer climates. The horses' winter coats appeared earlier than usual—Nature had set her stage for the last act."

Why did these men stay in Montana after that cataclysmic winter of 1886-87? The story of "Prairie Dog" Arnold, as told by Howard, might provide a partial answer.

This painting by Charles Russell depicts the victims of the 1886-87 drought.

Arnold came west as a young man, but was painlessly separated from his bankroll by cardsharpers. He found himself broke in a strange town. He could have wired home for money, but instead, he decided to do something nobody had ever thought of. He began snaring prairie dogs, put them in boxes, and sold them as pets to the first tourists, who were a gullible lot.

Ultimately, Arnold became a prosperous rancher, and always took to the trail with his riders.

On one trip, while camped near a good spring, one of his cowboys returned from the water hole, shouting, "There's an Indian's head in that spring."

"Damn it," said Arnold, an insatiable collector of Indian relics, "I forgot about that head. I put it in the spring last year to peel it and intended to get it out before you boys showed up."

Another pioneer choosing Montana was Granville Stuart, a Virginian and one of the first in Montana Territory to engage in the beef business.

In 1860, Stuart brought some lame oxen in from Idaho Territory, fattened them in western Montana, and a year later drove them back and resold them. The beef market in the mining camps was hot and growing rapidly.

A Montana blizzard was no fun in which to hunt cattle.
(Drawing by W.H.D. Koerner)

There was also Pierre Wibaux, a wealthy member of a French textile family, who came to Montana in 1883 to start a cattle business. According to author Howard, the disaster of 1886-87 wiped Wibaux out, but he returned to France to seek some capital, found it, and started his operation again.

He lived to see his cattle herds grow to seventy five thousand head as he bought out cattlemen that were going broke and leaving Montana.

Because of the drought throughout the west, cattlemen began moving their animals to Montana, seeking grass. Following the severe drought of 1885, The *Rocky Mountain Husbandman* angered the cattlemen when it printed:

> *"The range of the past is gone; that of the present is of little worth and cannot be relied on in the future. Range husbandry is over, is ruined, is*

103

destroyed—it may have been (caused)
by the insatiable greed of its followers."

The cattlemen retorted angrily. What could they have done? There was not enough hay in the United States to feed the immense herds on the Great Plains.

Granville Stuart said, "There was no way of preventing the overstocking of the ranges as they were free to all. But the range business is no longer a reasonably safe business, it is from this time on a gamble, with the trump cards in the hands of the elements."

In January 1885, the *Chicago Times* printed this special dispatch from Montana's cowboy capital, Miles City:

> *"The whole valley on all sides of*
> *Miles City is filled with cattle, seeking*
> *what protection the scant shrubbery*
> *affords. Even in the streets of the town*
> *great droves of cattle wander back and*
> *forth, but there is no food for them."*

Losses were mounting, but still new herds were being crowded onto the Montana range. "The bonanza days were gone," Howard wrote, "and some of the old-timers recognized that fact.

Some stockmen and cowboys stay, even though life was hard. The stayed because it was a free way of life.

It was obvious the days of the range cowboy were coming to an end. Cowboys, who had been "line riders" in the first days of the open range, patrolling an unmarked boundary based on creeks or imaginary lines drawn from distant buttes, became fence riders.

They carried wire cutters and pliers to replace the six shooters in their belt scabbards, said Howard.

Finally they degenerated into haying hands, or they quit.

Most of them were traditionally hostile to any form of labor that could not be performed from a horse's back, and they quit rather than degrade themselves.

Chapter 15

The Range Wars

> "*If you have not already learned you are now made to understand that wool and mutton are as necessary as 'beef and broad brimmed hats and revolvers.'*"

The bitter conflict between cattlemen and sheepmen covered nearly five decades in which more than fifty humans and some fifty-three thousand sheep were killed.

This conflict began in Texas and Colorado but spread to other territories where cattlemen objected to the entry of sheep onto their ranges.

Most cowboys disliked the sheepherders as much as their bosses did. A cowboy that was sympathetic to the sheepmen was called a "*sheep dipper.*"

As the cattle ranges in Texas became overstocked in the 1880s, violence increased between the sheepmen and cattlemen. When the arctic winter of 1886-87 caused cattle to die by the thousands, the open range way of doing business pretty much ended.

Cattlemen realized that if they wanted to succeed, they had to be in both the land business as well as the cattle business. Consequently, competition for the remaining public domain became intense. Cattle ranchers, small stockmen, homesteaders, and sheepmen all vied for the properties available.

The number of sheep increased slowly but steadily across the west. Simple economic reality favored sheep ranching. Sheep produced two products, wool and mutton, and both could produced more economically than beef. Sheep could subsist on range that would not support cattle. Sheep could live on sagebrush and sparse upland grasses and they required a third less water than cattle needed.

Another factor was that investment in a sheep operation was considerably less than that for an efficient cattle operation.

Wool being hauled to market in Texas
(Texas State Archives, Austin)

One of the men who realized the benefits of sheep ranching was Bryant B. Brooks, a pioneer Wyoming cattle rancher who was also the state's governor from 1905 to 1911.

According to Bill O'Neal, in his book, *Cattlemen vs. Sheepherders*, Brooks soon discovered that sheep brought year-round jobs to Wyoming and a steadier measure of prosperity than other agricultural enterprises.

Brooks decided that he too would enter the sheep business. He bought a band of three thousand sheep in Denver. The band had not been shorn nor had they yet lambed. Brooks realized a handsome profit, which encouraged him to invest more heavily in sheep.

Another thing that came home to Brooks was the fact that sheep were less injurious to the range than were cattle. "Cattle graze over the same range all the year and feed differently from sheep, invariably eating the coarser, taller grasses first, thereby destroying the seed stalks so the ranges do not reseed. Sheep eat the flowers, weeds, and fine grass first, and let the stalks alone."

This photo shows sheep that were clubbed to death near Tie Siding, Wyoming.
(Courtesy American Heritage Center, University of Wyoming, Laramie)

Many cattlemen, however, refused to have anything to do with the detested sheep, and some of them were so adamant as to wage war against the sheepmen.

These attacks were usually aimed at isolated sheep camps. The attackers were mounted cowboys who often wore masks, sometimes made of gunnysacks. *Gunnysackers* became a common name for these marauders.

While most of the sheep were shot, there were times when the animals were clubbed with ax handles or wagon wheel spokes. Some of the sheep did not die outright but had their backs broken or were otherwise maimed.

In Colorado, sheepmen were quick to rebel when a cattlemen's organization in Pueblo County announced that sheep would have to be confined to certain ranges.

The sheepmen issued their own strong statement:

"If you have not already learned you are now made to understand that wool and mutton are as necessary as 'beef and broad brimmed hats and revolvers.'"

The statement of the sheepmen was ignored, for when sheep rancher A.D. Robinson brought twenty four hundred head of sheep into Las Animas County, adjacent to Pueblo and Huerfano counties, eight or ten men struck, killing and wounding a considerable number.

War after war was reported throughout the range country where cattlemen and sheepmen were pitted against each other.

It was in Wyoming where cattlemen put up their strongest defense to keep sheep from taking over their ranges. The Wyoming Stock Growers Association commanded a powerful position in territorial affairs. The WSGA had an annual budget of $52,796, compared to the entire territorial budget of $38,000.

Battlegrounds in Wyoming included courtrooms as well as rangelands. There was a brief lull in the range war when entire herds of cattle were left dead or during the arctic winter of 1886-87.

Many of the ranchers were forced out of business, leaving a devastated Wyoming Stock Growers Association. Its membership dropped from four hundred sixteen members in 1886 to just sixty-eight members in 1890.

Sheep ranchers quickly filled the void left by the devastation of cattle by the freezing winter. Some cattlemen also decided they would be better off raising sheep than they would cattle.

By 1900, the Wyoming Stock Growers Association was revived and again cattlemen became a force in the state. They again resisted the sheepmen and "nesters" that were occupying good rangeland. Stockmen also suspected that some of the cattle being raised by the farmers came from their herds.

The cattlemen decided to take strong action against rustlers of their cattle. One incident concerned Emma Watson, known as

110

"Cattle Kate." Kate ran a bawdy house, and was known to trade her favors for rustled cattle. Her partner, Jim Averell, was brought to trial for shooting a ranch foreman in the leg.

Cattle Kate and Averell were warned to leave the county, and in addition a rustling charge was lodged against Averell. The two were hanged from a tree on July 20, 1889.

Convictions of seven men in Wyoming for the murder of five sheepherders on April 2, 1909 pretty much brought a close to the cattlemen-sheepmen wars. There were later scattered events, but by the 1920s, both sides stopped using vigilante methods to solve range rights.

Stockmen, both growers of sheep and of cattle, resorted to their state legislators to bring order to the range.

Chapter 16

The Cowboy Hat

> Stetson then fashioned the fur into a big hat, one that would protect a wearer from rain, sun, cold, wind and even hail. His compatriots were impressed.

No other thing so strongly depicts the "Cowboy" image as does the hat he wears.

John Batterson Stetson was one of 12 children of Stephen and Susan Balderson Stetson. Born in Orange, New Jersey in 1830, John left school early to learn the hatter's trade in his father's hat shop.

Stetson's *Boss of the Plains* hat.

Following his father's death, John continued to work for his older brothers. He bought the raw materials, he made hats, taught others how to make hats and he sold hats. His brothers took the profits.

Stetson considered opening his own shop. He was stopped from doing so when he was stricken with tuberculosis, probably from the fumes exuded by the mercury compound used in hat manufacture. It was in 1865, with one hundred dollars to his name, that John opened his hat company in Philadelphia.

His only chance at beating the disease, he told himself, was to get out in the open. He moved to St. Joseph, Missouri and went to work molding bricks. He soon was manager of the brickyard and then a partner.

113

His fortune turned bleak when the Missouri River flooded everything. A half-million bricks, ready to be baked, melted into the silt of the rushing river and floated downstream. The river carried Stetson's job with it.

Adapted from David Dary's book, *Cowboy Culture*

Without work and looking for something to do, Stetson tried to enlist in the Civil War. He was turned down because of his physical disabilities.

Young John was invited to accompany a party of men outfitting for a trek to Pike's Peak, where they would prospect for gold. He decided to go.

When a storm unleashed on the hiking party, the men rushed to lash animal skins together to serve as tent shelters. Since the skins were not tanned, they ruined under the soaking rain and had to be discarded.

Once as the party was bedding down, someone remarked, "Too bad there isn't some easier way to make tent cloth."

"There is," said Stetson, "by felting."

Felting is a process that dates back centuries before Christ. Although a strand of animal fur appears smooth to the naked eye, it is actually covered with scales. When clean fur is matted together, the scales interlock. If the mat is alternately dipped in hot water and then squeezed, the scales lock even more tightly, forming the material called felt.

Instead of trying to explain the concept to his companions, Stetson gave a demonstration. He sharpened his axe to a razor's edge and used it to shave the fur off several hides. With a hickory sapling and a leather thong, he made a bow and began agitating the fur, keeping it in the air until the long hairs and dirt were separated.

He then sprayed water over the fur. In a few minutes, he had a mat that could be lifted. Stetson dipped this in boiling water. As it began to shrink, he manipulated it, squeezing out excess water until he had a soft blanket of felt.

Stetson then fashioned the fur into a big hat, one that would protect a wearer from rain, sun, cold, wind and even hail. His compatriots were impressed.

After reaching Pike's Peak, Stetson soured on mining very fast. It was hard work for pitifully little money. Nevertheless, he hung around the mining camps and his felt hat became the talk of the miners.

A horseman rode into camp one day and spotted Stetson's fur hat. He asked to try it on. Stetson liked the picture he saw of the man wearing his hat. Here was a giant of a man, sitting in a silver-ornamented saddle on a spirited horse, wearing his hat.

The horseman liked the effect too, and gave John a five dollar gold piece for the hat.

John decided to return to Philadelphia and get into the hat business again. He used the only one hundred dollars he had to buy hat-making tools, and to rent a small room where he once again, began making hats.

His first design did not sell well. It was simply a copy of the style in vogue in Philadelphia at the time. He realized to be successful he would have to make a hat that was different. Pondering his position, Stetson then asked himself, "Why not sell hats somewhere else?"

He couldn't forget the hatted horseman that bought the hat from him in the Pikes Peak mining camps. As he pondered the image over and over in his mind, he realized what the horseman looked like wearing his hat. He looked like a cattle baron.

The cattle business was a new enterprise, and Stetson knew that cattlemen didn't wear any kind of distinguishing hat. He thought cattlemen might be receptive to something new and distinctive that would give them their own identity.

He made a hat from soft felt, the best he could find. He called the hat "Boss of the Plains."

The "Boss of the Plains" was a big, natural-colored hat, with a four-inch brim and a four-inch crown. It had a strap for a hatband. It could be said that Stetson's hat was a modified Mexican sombrero.

Stetson's hat caught on with the cattlemen who wanted a hat that could withstand both pounding rain and burning sun.

He quickly decided to mass market the "Boss of the Plains". Stetson obtained a list of every hat dealer in the southwest and sent each one a sample hat, along with a letter asking for an order.

Stetson knew this was a calculated risk that could either make him or break him. To obtain raw materials, he had to go into debt. Within two weeks the orders started coming in. Some dealers even sent cash with their orders in an attempt to get preferential treatment and expedited orders.

It wasn't long before a big Stetson hat was the pride of the cowboy. The broad brim shielded him from the sun and the rain. He could wave it above his head and turn cattle during a roundup or a stampede.

In case of emergency, he could even carry oats in the crown to feed his horse. He could dip up water that was inaccessible to his horse and let his horse drink from his hat. The hat came in handy to fan a campfire, as well.

There was no stopping the Stetson. It became the best-known hat west of the Mississippi River. Everybody wore them, wealthy ranchers, storekeepers, preachers and U.S. marshals.

Stack-A-Lee
By Frank Hutchinson

Hawlin Alley on a dark and drizzly night,
Billy Lyons and Stack-A-Lee had one terrible fight.
All about that Hat.

Stack-A-Lee walked to the barroom, and he called for a glass of beer.
Turned around to Billy Lyons, said, "What are you doin' here?"
"Waitin' for a train, please bring my woman home.

"Stack-A-Lee, oh Stack-A-Lee, please don't take my life.
Got three little children and a-weepin', lovin' wife.
You're a bad man, bad man, Stack-A-Lee."

"God bless your children and I'll take care of your wife.
You stole my John B., now I'm bound to take your life."
All about that John B. Stetson hat.

Stack-A-Lee turned to Billy Lyons and he shot him right through the head.
Only taking one shot to kill Billy Lyons dead.
All about that John B. Stetson hat.

Sent for the doctor, well the doctor he did come,
Just pointed out Stack-A-Lee, said, "Now what have you done?
You're a bad man, bad man, Stack-A-Lee."

Six big horses and a rubber-tired hack,
Taking him to the cemetery, but they failed to bring him back.
All about that John B. Stetson hat.

Hawlin Alley, thought I heard the bulldogs bark-
It must have been old Stack-A-Lee stumbling in the dark.
He's a bad man, gonna land him right back in jail.

Well they got old Stack-A-Lee and they laid him right back in jail.
Couldn't get a man around to go Stack-A-Lee's bail.
All about that John B. Stetson hat.

Stack-A-Lee turned to the jailer, he said, "Jailer, I can't sleep.
Round my bedside Billy Lyons began to creep."
All about that John B. Stetson hat.

Broncobusters

Not all cowboys were highly skilled horsemen. Standing out above and most admired by the rest was the man who broke the wild horses.

Harsh *gaucho* methods of breaking horses often caused injury to the animals. Horses were so plentiful that death or injury to the animals was of little concern. The ranch manager simply salvaged the horsehides.

The Argentine dictator Juan Manuel de Rosas owned a number of ranches in the province of Buenos Aires. He paid his broncobusters fifty percent more than his other gauchos. At a taming session on his San Martin Ranch in 1846, riders killed seven of the seventy-five horses they were taming.

A German visiting California in 1842 was shocked at the treatment vaqueros used on their mounts. "The barbarous Californians look upon the horse as a useful commodity which is of little value and easily replaced."

Vaqueros considered it unmanly to break or ride a mare. Riding a female horse was considered unmanly.

A good hand in early California might earn twelve dollars a month. The tamer would earn twenty dollars.

Bronco busting took its toll on both cowboys and horses. Richard Slatta, in his book "Cowboys of the Americas," said, "In the American West men who 'snapped broncs' did not have long careers, but smarter 'peelers' developed their own special techniques.

These techniques ranged from riding in deep sand, as William Henry Sears did in Colorado, to riding the horses in the surf, as in the case off paniolos.

Chapter 17

Trouble in Paradise

> The king then placed a *kapu* (royal sacred protection) on the cattle. The animals were then allowed to run wild.

Cattle arrived in Hawaii in 1793 as gifts from England in 1793 to Hawaiian King Kamehameha.

When English Captain George Vancouver delivered the animals to the king, he extracted a promise from the king that there would be no killing of the animals for ten years. There were eight females and four males in the number. One male and one female died shortly after landing.

The king then placed a *kapu* (royal sacred protection) on the cattle. The animals were then allowed to run wild.

It wasn't realized what damage these beasts could do.

By the 1830s, herds of wild cattle roamed the major islands. The animals were allowed free run of the hills and forests.

In 1830, a *kapu* was placed on sandalwood, forbidding its harvest. Unfortunately, the *kapu* came too late. The sandalwood was almost entirely gone. Helping to decimate Hawaii's forests were the whalers that wastefully stripped thousands of acres of forests for firewood.

Later, early sugar cane growers added to the problem by consuming large quantities of firewood in their processing mills.

A District Commissioner for North Kohala at the time noted that birds, which preferred the cool, moist understory of the native forests, were deserting the areas opened by cutting.

Around the middle of the nineteenth century, alarms sounded from a variety of sources. These alarms were about the effects the cattle were having on Hawaii's lands and forests.

In 1856, Abraham Fornander, editor of the Sandwich Islands' Monthly Magazine, criticized the free-roaming beasts. He argued that cattle had altered the very climate of Waimea. The cattle had destroyed the thick wood that as recently as 1825 stretched across the North Hawaii plain.

In 1835, botanist David Douglas met an untimely death on the eastern slopes of Mauna Kea. Officially he had fallen in a cattle trap occupied by a wild bull and was gored to death. It was also found that an English convict lived in the forest nearby, and he trapped wild animals for hides and meat.

It was never determined if Douglas' death was accidental or not. A sum of money that Douglas was carrying was never found, and some disbelieve that an expert wilderness traveler such as Douglas could have fallen into a cattle trap.

Another critic was William Hillebrand, surgeon at the Queen's Hospital, and a pioneer in Hawaiian botany. In an 1856 address to the Royal Hawaiian Agricultural Society, Hillebrand said, "Of all the destroying influences man brings to bear upon nature, cattle is the worst."

In truth, cattle did decimate the natural fauna. Today, whole slopes of mountains behind Honolulu are blanketed with eucalyptus, with nary a native to be seen. Foresters, a century ago sought to cover the lands denuded by cattle with the fastest growing trees they could find—that is eucalyptus.

Hawaiian cowboys were forced to work around water as cattle had to be transported by small boat from land to steamships. They tied the horse of the animals to the gunwales and then hoisted them aboard the steamer in a sling.　　(Bishop Museum, Honolulu)

Chapter 18

The Paniolo: *Hawaiian Cowboy*

"Our paniolo had to catch wild cattle. They would set up ropers at the edge of a *kipuka* (a densely overgrown piece of land entirely surrounded by newer lava). They'd only get one swing of the lasso to catch a longhorn or it would get away.

Hawaii's cowboy history is strong and goes back a long ways. English explorer Captain George Vancouver brought longhorn cattle from Santa Barbara, California to Hawaii in 1793 and presented them as gifts to King Kamehameha.

The king turned the animals loose to run wild. He also placed a *kapu* (royal sacred protection) on them. They demolished forestland, and in some places, drove out the natives by trampling the unfenced taro patches and truck gardens.

Little use was made of the interior or semi-barren uplands on Hawaii Island before John Palmer Parker, an American, started a small ranch in Kohala. Parker Ranch's story begins in 1809 when 19-year old John jumped ship and became acquainted with King Kamehameha.

Parker became the first man in Hawaii that was allowed to slay some of the thousands of cattle that roamed the island's plains and valleys, all descendents of the five head of cattle given to Kamehameha by British Captain George Vancouver.

Due mostly to Parker's efforts, beef replaced sandalwood as the Big Island's chief export. Parker's wealth and influence grew, and in 1815 he married the daughter of a high-ranking chief. The couple had two sons and a daughter, thus starting the Parker family dynasty in Hawaii.

These cowboys are working cattle on the Parker Ranch on the big island of Hawaii. Photo courtesy of Parker Ranch   (Photo by Bob Fewell)

Parker, born in Newton, Massachusetts in 1790, settled at Waimea, Hawaii in 1815. His job for the king was to shoot the wild cattle, prepare their hides, and salt the beef for sale to visiting ships.

The Hawaiian style of ranching included capturing wild bullocks and driving them into pits dug in the forest floor. The animals were left until they were somewhat tamed by hunger and thirst.

Paniolos then dragged them out of the pits. The horns of the animals were tied to the horns of a tame steer that knew the direction to the paddock where food and water was available.

With skillful management, Parker built the cattle business into the great 175,000-acre Parker Ranch, the second largest ranch under the American flag. The King Ranch in Texas is the largest.

California vaqueros, the Spanish *paniolos*, were persuaded to come to Hawaii to teach the Hawaiians how to ride and rope. The paniolos adopted Mexican techniques and dress to suit his local conditions.

For example, the Hawaiian cowboy retained the general shape of the Spanish felt sombrero worn by the vaquero, but the paniolos altered the materials from which the hat was made. Instead of felt, the paniolo used the leaves of the *hala* (pandanus tree or screw pine). They called their hat a *papale*.

The paniolo added their own touches to the their cowboy head gear. They decorated their hats with richly hued local shells and feathers.

One old paniolo defended the islander use of the lei. "Even the roughest, toughest, rowdiest, most rugged and most manly wear lei. We do it for the pure joy and pleasure of it and you cannot tell me that we don't look handsome as men should."

Hawaiians quickly adapted to this dashing sport. The king owned all of the wild herds, and the right to slaughter was let out on contract. The king, in the early 1800's, met with 245 chiefs. Under a program known as the *Great Mahele*, he divided the land.

The lands that he kept for himself and his family were called crown lands. The divisions that he reserved for the government were known as government lands. The land that he gave to the chiefs to own forever was called the *konohiki* lands.

The king made separate arrangements with each chief. All these arrangements by the king were recorded in a book called the *Mahele* (division) book. It took many months to complete this process, but when finally complete, the division book was known as the *Great Mahele*.

This was a good start on reforming the land system. It meant the government now owned some land, and the government could now sell or barter its land and make some money. Just maybe, the government could sell land and pay off the national debt, and put some money into the school system.

The Great Mahele did not solve all of the land problems. Most of the people of Hawaii were not chiefs. Consequently, most of the people of Hawaii were still without any land.

In the 1850s, Hawaii began importing breeding cattle, both Aberdeen Angus and Hereford. A Durham bull was imported in 1854 and Devon cattle in 1855.

There was estimated forty thousand head of cattle in Hawaii at that time. As late as 1875, hides and tallow was worth more than the meat. About one-fourth of all land in the islands today is still pasture.

Many of the pastures in Hawaii were so waterless; the cows grew up there without ever getting a real drink of water. The animals existed on the heavy dews that clung to the grass each morning.

Parker Ranch, on the Big Island of Hawaii, is one of the largest ranches in the United States and home of Hawaii's cowboy, or *paniolo*. Paniolos are a tough, hard-riding breed of cowboy that worked six generations at the Parker Ranch. The ranch owns approximately 175,000 acres, 250 horses and 30,000 to 35,000 head of cattle.

One of those Hawaiian paniolos was Ikua Purdy, who stunned Americans when he won the 1908 World Roping Championship in Cheyenne, Wyoming. Hawaiians sing his praises and boast about his skills in cowboy songs and hulas.

The Paniolo Preservation Society inducted Ikua into its hall of fame, but the National Rodeo Cowboy Hall of Fame has skipped over the famed paniolo.

Ikua was born on Christmas Eve, December 24, 1873 in Waimea. The second son of nine children, he was the great-grandson of John Palmer Parker. He learned to ride and rope on the grasslands of upland forests of Waimea and Mauna Kea.

When he competed in Cheyenne, Ikua and his fellow paniolos found the weather troubling. They weren't used to the cold. Ikua and the other paniolos created quite a stir with their odd slouched hats and colorful hatbands, peculiar saddles and bright shirts.

They created even more of a curiosity by speaking a language completely foreign to the American cowboys—they talked in native Hawaiian.

Few American cowboys gave the paniolos a chance at the Cheyenne event. These strangers were riding borrowed mounts and the horse and rider had hardly become acquainted. The rope horses they were able to borrow were considered inferior and lacking in speed.

It's not surprising that Wyoming hosts were caught off-guard when Ikua roped his steer in fifty-six seconds flat to win the 1908 steer roping championship.

Eben Low, a Hawaiian rancher, knew very well that Ikua might do well at Cheyenne and he secured the invitation for the paniolo to attend. Eben later explained why he thought Ikua could be a winner.

"Our paniolo had to catch wild cattle. They would set up ropers at the edge of a *kipuka* (a densely overgrown piece of land entirely surrounded by newer lava). The cattle would run on the fly and the cowboys had to be ready with horses in good condition.

"They'd only get one swing of the lasso to catch a longhorn or it would get away," said Low. "The paniolo had to catch fast-running cattle. It's what they did everyday."

Chapter 19

Cowboy Humor

> *Shorty didn't know whether to feed or starve his cold so he drowned it.*

Ranchers used all of their ingenuity to come up with a cattle brand that couldn't be changed by rustlers.

One story told is about the rancher who used his initials, "*IC*" for his brand. He later found some of his cattle branded with *ICU*.

After recovering the cattle, they were rebranded with *ICU2*.

When a Texas ranch held a dance one rainy evening, the owners of a distant spread came with their newly hired governess, who forgot her overshoes when she and her employers left for home.

An eager cowboy showed up the following Sunday and presented the young lady, whose name was Anne, with a parcel containing one overshoe.

"But there were two," She said.

"Yes, I know it," replied the cowboy. "I'll bring the other one next Sunday, if you don't mind, and, Miss Anne, I sure wish you was a centipede."

A cowboy stopped at Charles Goodnight's JA Ranch looking for work. The gruff Mr. Goodnight was in his small fruit orchard near his ranch house planting trees.

The cowboy asked for a job punching cattle. Goodnight kept on digging without answering. Frustrated, the cowboy picked up a shovel and started digging along with the rancher. A dinner bell rang and Goodnight asked the cowboy to join him and the others.

After eating, Goodnight, followed by the cowboy, went back to the orchard. "He never did hire me," the cowboy said, but he put me on the payroll."

Some people just simply didn't like cowboys. Bill Nye, a Laramie, Wyoming newspaper writer, was one of them.

He wrote: "The cowboy was generally a youth who thinks he will not earn his twenty-five dollars per month if he does not yell and whoop and shoot, and scare little girls into St. Vitus' dance. I've known more cowboys to injure themselves with their own revolvers than to injure anyone else. This is evidently because they are more familiar with the hoe than they are with the Smith & Wesson.

A cowboy from New Mexico rode into Tombstone, Arizona, before law had come to the town. He was riding a magnificent stallion.

He passed the word that the stallion was for sale for half what it was really worth. He soon found a purchaser who paid him in full for the horse.

"What about the bill of sale," the buyer asked.

"Oh, don't worry about the horse's title as long as you go west with him. But don't take him east. It's not so good in that direction."

♦♦♦

A tenderfoot cowboy arrived in a frontier town and decided to enter a game of poker with a grizzled old prospector.

Hand after hand, the tenderfoot received good hands. When he was dealt four aces, he knew he was a sure winner and laid his hand open on the table and reached for the pot.

"Hold on," the prospector said, "I'll take care of the pot."

"But I've got four aces," the cowboy said.

"Yes," the prospector said, "but I've got a looloo."

"A looloo?" asked the cowboy. "What's a looloo?"

"Any three clubs with two diamonds," said the prospector. "See the sign on the wall."

Sure enough, a cardboard sign on the back wall said, "A looloo beats four aces."

"Well," I'm still game," said the tenderfoot. After a few minutes, a big smile crossed the cowboy's face. "I've got a looloo," he said, laying his cards face up.

The miner shook his head. "This is really too bad. Look at the sign behind you."

The tenderfoot turned and saw the cardboard sign: THE LOOLOO CAN BE PLAYED BUT ONCE IN A NIGHT.

In Cheyenne, Wyoming, Colonel Luke Murrin, who served as city magistrate and judge, figured out a way to take care of his bar tab.

Everyone charged with gunplay that was brought before Judge Murrin was fined ten dollars. To these fines, the judge added twenty-five cents:

"Your fine is ten dollars and two bits."

"Yes, your Honor, but what's the two bits for?"

"To buy your honorable judge a drink in the morning."

A Tucson, Arizona judge named Meyers had no legal training and was unable to obtain any legal books.

Before being appointed judge, Meyers had been a pharmacist. To lend dignity to his office, he placed his largest volumes of materia medica, dispensatories, and military hygiene, as well as a copy of Webster's dictionary on his desk.

Whenever a difficult case came before him, Meyers would consult one of these books, deliberate a few moments, and then render a verdict.

In still another Arizona case, a judge noticed after two hours of preliminaries that there were only eleven jurors present. "Where is the twelfth juryman?" the judge demanded to know.

"Please, your honor," replied one of the eleven jurors seated, "he had to go back to his ranch. But he left his verdict with me."

Chapter 20

The Hanging of Cattle Kate

> Kate's cattle herd kept growing at a mysterious rate. Neighboring cattlemen believed it was because admiring cowboys in Averell's saloon were receiving personal favors from Kate in exchange for beef on the hoof.

When Ella Watson first arrived in Rawlins, Wyoming, she worked at the Rawlins House. She worked as a cook and a domestic for two years. Because the establishment was thought to be a brothel, she was labeled a prostitute.

Jim Averell established a homestead, and, because he was situated in proximity to the Oregon and Mormon trails, opened a general store and saloon. He was also appointed postmaster and notary public.

During his trips to Rawlins, Jim and Kate, who would later become widely known as "Cattle Kate," became infatuated with each other. The couple traveled to Lander, Wyoming, presumably to get married. It is unclear

Ella "Cattle Kate" Watson was lynched by a group of Wyoming cattlemen who claimed she was rustling cattle from them. (University of Wyoming)

whether a marriage ever took place. Many think the trip to

Lander was in order for Kate to file for a homestead near that of Jim Averell's.

Because only one homestead per family was permitted, it is likely that Jim and Kate never said any marriage vows.

Kate's cattle herd kept growing at a mysterious rate. Neighboring cattlemen believed it was because admiring cowboys in Averell's saloon were receiving personal favors from Kate in exchange for beef on the hoof, beef that belong to the neighboring ranchers.

In the fall of 1888, Ellen bought twenty head of footsore cattle from a trail driver. When she applied for a brand, her application was rejected for unknown reasons. Kate then bought an existing brand, the L U from another rancher and branded the cattle she had bought from the trail driver.

On July 20, 1889 a stock detective named George Henderson rode through Ellen's pasture and saw cattle with the L U brand. He notified Albert Bothwell, a wealthy cattle rancher that neighbored Ellen's property. "Though Bothwell, no doubt, knew that Ellen had had those cattle for almost a year, he seized on the situation as a chance to get rid of Jim Averell and Ellen Watson.

Albert John Bothwell was a neighbor of Ellen. He also wanted her land and water rights. He approached Ellen several times with offers, but she invariable refused.

Bothwell had run-ins, too, with Jim Averell, even though the homesteader had given the rancher a right of way through his property that allowed Bothwell to irrigate his pastureland.

Based on what detective Henderson had told him, Bothwell called for a meeting the Wyoming Stock Growers Association to discuss the newly branded cattle on Ellen's property. Six of the men decided to take matters into their own hands. Other cattlemen wanted nothing to do with it.

Claiming they had warrants to arrest them, the six ranchers converged on Jim's roadhouse and took Ellen and Jim captive. The six ranchers were A.J. Bothwell, John Durbin, Robert

Conner, E.F. McLean, Tom Sun, and a man named Galbrath. The couple was hung from a tree near the Sweetwater River.

According to her grand nephew, Daniel W. (Watson) Brumbaugh, little of what has been written about Cattle Kate is true.

"There have been several books and magazines written about Ellen Watson, known by them as *Cattle Kate"*, said Brumbaugh. "Several of these authors never really researched her life. They just took what the newspapers said about her in the days of her lynching for granted and wrote about her from the articles."

Brumbaugh was especially critical of the newspaper in Cheyenne, Wyoming. "The newspaper at that time belonged to the powerful organization known as the Wyoming Stock Growers Association. They controlled the newspaper and its printing.

"They printed what they wanted the public to hear, not the real facts about her life and what really took place at her lynching. They fabricated the lives of three women into one. The editor of the Cheyenne newspaper wrote the incident like you would a dime store novel."

Brumbaugh said Ella's own father told her siblings never to speak of her name again after he attended her inquest in Wyoming in August 1889.

Not one of them ever spoke of her name after that, he said, even to their own children, though some of them tried to get their parents to tell them about their oldest aunt.

Brumbaugh, however, could not let the issue rest. "I have been on the homestead site in Smith County, Kansas that her father homesteaded in November 1877 where Ellen lived until she married. I have traveled to Rawlins, Wyoming where she filed for her claim. I have researched in the local courthouse in that city for her records.

"I have been to the homestead site on the Pathfinder Ranch and the lynching site and seen the tree from which the cattlemen lynched her and Jim Averell. I have sent off to the

National Archives for her homestead filings. I do know something about her life since I am related to her."

Brumbaugh added, "Only one of the lynchers knew Ellen Watson well. He lived within a mile of Ellen's homestead place. He lied and fabricated stories about Jim and Ellen so he could get rid of them and finally get their land and water rights."

According to her Estate Administrator, the cattle did belong to her, and he sued the Durbin Cattle Company and A.J. Bothwell for compensation for her estate, said Brumbaugh.

He detailed Ellen's early life: "Ellen Liddy Watson was born out of wedlock in July 1860. Her mother Frances was born in Dromore, County Down Ireland, and came to Canada with her parents and her other siblings around 1858. Since they were pure Irish, the fact of an unwed mother probably brought shame upon the family at that time.

"On February 24, 1886, Ellen was going towards the courthouse in Rawlins, when she met this handsome young man. He introduced himself as James Averell. He told her he had a roadhouse that had an eating place and a general store. He also had a bar where cowboys or anybody else could have a drink. He told Ellen about some land adjoining his that she could probably homestead."

Ellen Watson and Jim Averell later drove to Lander, Wyoming and applied for a marriage license. The marriage license was never returned. Years later, after the lynching, John Fales, a neighbor of Ellen, said the couple was engaged. They intended to get married after Ellen proved up on her homestead claim.

After the hanging, the bodies of Ellen and Jim were brought back to Jim's roadhouse. They were buried on Jim's ranch.

When the six accused ranchers were brought before a grand jury, the case was not heard because of a lack of witnesses. The only witness, a young boy, was killed a few weeks before the scheduled hearing.

While circumstantial evidence certainly points a finger at the six cattlemen as the murderers of Jim Averell and Ella Watson,

138

it is unlikely that conclusive evidence will ever materialize. The case still lives in the minds of many in Wyoming.

Chapter 21

Texas Fever

Settlers guarded their property with rifles to prevent the Texas cattle from coming too close. Cattle breeders as far east as New York saw their purebred stock die when Texas Longhorns were shipped into the state.

The period of the Texas cattle drives was short but the drives caused considerable conflict between the cowboys and the settlers they passed.

A disease scientifically called *bovine babesia bigemina* was causing cattle in areas where the trail herds passed to sicken and often die. It was called Texas fever. When the disease was blamed on the trail herds, it infuriated the Texans.

"If our cattle are carrying the disease, then why aren't they sick? It's only northern cattle that are dying," said the Texans.

Even though the Texas longhorn appeared perfectly healthy, it became clear in states such as Missouri that the disease hitting their cattle came from the Texas herds as they traveled through the territory.

A Missouri veterinarian wrote, "From the first breaking out of this fever, it was found to be confined to the large roads or highways running through from south to north, and finally was centered on Texas cattle."

The outbreak of cattle fever in the East and Midwest directly affected the trail drives. Nobody wanted the Texas cattle and soon there were no buyers for the herds in Abilene. Soon there was a glut of cattle for one hundred miles around Abilene. All the grass was eaten down to the bare ground.

Some states set up laws to prevent Texas cattle from going through because of the tick fever they spread. The disease didn't affect the Texas cattle.

Drawing from book, "We Pointed Them North"

Unknowingly, Texas cattle were carrying fever ticks northward to cattle that had no resistance to the "Texas Tick Fever," or *babesiosis*. While the longhorns had developed resistance to Texas fever, infected fever ticks transmitted the protozoal blood disease to animal without this resistance.

The states crossed by the Texas trail herds took actions to protect their own cattle. Missouri passed a law to prevent cattle from Texas from entering the state. Kansas made it illegal to drive Texas cattle to Abilene. The Chisholm Trail, which ended in Abilene, closed and was never used again.

Violence occasionally broke out when a trail herd edged too close to Colorado cattle. These skirmishes led to the organization of the Colorado Cattlemen's Association, which pledged that no Texas herds could pass between Arkansas and the South Platte rivers unless they had been within the territory for at least a year.

Attempts to restrict the Texas cattle herds eventually left only a narrow strip up the Kansas-Colorado line open for trail herds to travel. Texans sometimes defied the quarantines, which

Cattle are being dipped in this 1915 photo to kill ticks on the Circle Ranche in Alberta, Canada.　(Glenbow Archives, Calgary)

they felt were simply to stop competition from their lower-priced cattle. These attempts led to shootings, hangings and arrests.

In 1892, fever tick outbreaks were rampant. The U.S. Secretary of Agriculture quarantined seven states, as well as parts of Texas and parts of five other states. Cattle destined for any purpose other than slaughter could be shipped northward from restricted regions only between November 15 and February 15, when the fever tick was apparently dormant.

In 1893 scientists at the Bureau of Animal Industry proved that Texas fever was spread from one cow to another by ticks, as many cattlemen had suspected.

Later research showed why longhorns from south Texas carried the disease without ill effects. Cattle first contracting the disease as calves do not become sick. They develop an immunity that persists for as long as the *babesia* germ remains in their blood.

Cattle remaining in the Texas fever area are continually reinfected and remain resistant. The resistance will last for several years, although the infected animals remain carriers of the disease.

About the time the cause of the disease was found, Robert J. Kleberg, of the King Ranch in Texas, developed a lime-sulphur dip to eliminate scabies, a mite that causes itching and mange. Kleberg noticed that many ticks died after his cattle were dipped.

Kleberg told Secretary of Agriculture Jeremiah M. Rusk, "Mr. Secretary, if the tick carries the disease, as your investigation seems to show, I will get rid of the tick."

The King Ranch manager set up facilities for trying experimental dips, and during a five-year span, twenty five thousand tick-infested cattle were passed through the vat to test the killing power of various concoctions.

In 1897, the Fort Worth Stockyards built a large dipping vat for additional chemical trials. In this same year, livestock commissioners from several states in conjunction with the U.S.

Bureau of Animal Industry set up uniform methods for tick inspection and quarantining of livestock.

By 1903, a dipping solution of arsenic, sal soda and pine tar was recommended, however the mixture demonstrated little success in slowing cattle losses.

Cattle were dropping like flies. Cattle losses amounted to forty million dollars per year by 1906. Strong-minded cattlemen convinced Congress to appropriate eighty five thousand five hundred dollars to support tick eradication in the southern states.

When the national eradication program kicked off, quarantines were slapped on one hundred ninety eight Texas counties, along with seven hundred twenty nine counties in other states.

In 1911, an arsenical dip, based on an Australian formula that was used in Cuba, became the "official dip." In five years, the eradication campaign was so successful that one hundred and twenty seven counties and portions of twenty other counties were released from quarantine.

It seems ironic, perhaps, that the discoveries leading to the eradication of Texas fever didn't come until the days of the cattle drives were past.

Chapter 22

The Canadian Cowboy

> "Never was a more respectable body of men maligned than the hard working, manly fellows who are found at work on properly conducted cattle ranches."

Borders don't seem to change the cowboy. One writer seemed to think that Canadian cowboys were a little better educated when it came to reading and writing, but both prided themselves on their ability to ride and perform ranch duties.

At Macleod, an early Alberta cowtown, a policeman complained in 1888 because he couldn't get anyone to dig a well. He was quickly informed that a man couldn't dig from the back of a horse.

Before European immigrants began arriving, Argentine ranchers were having the same difficulties in finding men that would work on foot.

If there is a difference in the reputation of Canadian cowboys and those in other parts of the west, it might be that Canadian riders were a little less inclined toward the "wild and wooly behavior" of his U.S. counterpart.

The *Calgary Herald* in 1884 contrasted the difference between cowboys of Canada and the United States:

> *The rough and festive cowboy of Texas and Oregon has no counterpart here. Two or three beardless lads wear jingling spurs and ridiculous revolvers and walk with a slouch,* (but) *the*

genuine   Alberta   cowboy   is   a gentleman."

Unlike other parts of the western frontier, the Royal Canadian Mounted police pretty much predated the cattle industry in Canada. Therefore guns played a much smaller role in Canada than they did in other parts of the American west.

Canadian saddle makers used the western stock saddle as their model.
(Glenbow Archives, Calgary)

It was a custom for Alberta cowboys to leave their guns at the livery stable with their horses and saddle gear.

"Guns were seldom carried on the range," said Herbert Church.

There was a difference in the language of cowboys south of the border to those in the north. A Texas cowboy would use the word "thrown" when a cowboy was bucked off a horse; A Saskatchewan would say, "piled".

148

A steer might be angry and stubborn to a Canadian cowboy, but to a Texan it would be "o'nery" or "ringy".

Cowboys on both sides of the border found the Stetson hat useful to fan the fire or dip up a drink from a stream, to shade a man's eyes or clap over the eyes of a bronc to gentle him down.

Another difference in cowboy lingo was the U.S. cowboy said "Rodeo", while the same event to a Canadian cowboy would be a "Stampede." Most things, such as the boots, bandanna, stock saddle, rope and the ways of breaking bronco were the same north and south.

Cattle ranching in western Canada began in the Fraser River valley of British Columbia. Americans trailed herds northward up the Okanagan Trail from Oregon. Eventually, the foothills and plains east of the Rockies in Alberta became the great open-range ranching area of Canada.

Mary Ella Inderwick, a rancher's wife in the foothills of the Canadian Rockies, wrote in a letter in 1884:

> *"We are in the foothills—no plains here—which all seems so near that one starts to ride to a certain land mark but finds oneself no nearer at the end of an hour."*

The Canadian cowboy faced many hazards on the Canadian prairie. Gopher holes that pocked the plains were hazards to both horse and man. McEachran said that prairie bred horses learned to avoid the holes.

A big complaint of Canadian cowboys, like their southern counterparts, was the attacks by "bulldog-flies" and mosquitoes. The bulldog-flies were described as bigger than a bee, which could make a large hole in the skin.

"These flies were very pertinacious, and the poor horses become frantic under their torment," said McEachran.

Cowboys from the United States rode north to Canada following the terrible blizzards of 1885-1886 where the expansion of the Alberta ranges made opportunities more attractive.

Author Richard Slatta, in his book, *Cowboys of the Americas*, quoted Canadian cowboy Fred Ings as saying, "...most of our best riders came from the States and they taught us all we know of cattle lore."

Bert Sheppard, of Longview, Alberta, talked of the differences between "real" horse training and rodeo bronc riding.

"The old unwritten code is that a horse should not be beaten over the head or spurred in the shoulder. Whereas the Rodeo rider receives marks of merit for spurring the shoulders, the bronco-buster stood a pretty good chance of getting 'fired' for doing it. Every thing in front of the cinch was supposed to belong to the horse."

One thing that could be said of cowboys on either side of the border was that they were usually honorable men.

It's haircut day. Is this cowboy going to town?
(Library of Congress)

Chapter 23

The Cattle Towns

> "The noisy fellow in exaggerated costume that rode up and down the streets whooping and shooting in the air was never a cowpuncher from any outfit. He was usually some 'would-be' bad man from the East decked out in paraphernalia from Montgomery Ward's of Chicago.
>
> (Granville Stuart in 1925)

Their very names stirred up trouble in one's mind; there was Abilene, Wichita, Dodge City, Ogalalla and Caldwell and Las Vegas in New Mexico, just to name a few.

These towns weren't much to look at. They often had dust up to ones ankles, and the board sidewalks were generally in disrepair. False front disguised the sleazy saloons, gambling dens and bordellos.

Ellsworth, Caldwell and Dodge City had the wildest reputations and had gained them well before they had become cattle towns. Railroad men, buffalo hunters, soldiers and camp followers generated the bad reputations of the towns more than cowboys.

When cowboys did come to town, they did spend money, and for this reason were welcomed as much by bookmakers, dry goods merchants, and grocers as they were by the saloons, gamblers and "shady ladies".

Abilene: It began as a small prairie village along the Smoky Hill Trail. It was laid out in 1861 near the crossing for Armistead Creek. Townsmen changed the name of the creek to "Mud" when Armistead joined the Confederate forces.

The name of Abilene comes from a verse in the New Testament, meaning, "City of the Plains". For years before the Texas trail drivers, the town was simply an assemblage of a half-dozen huts.

In 1867, Joseph McCoy had a vision for a great cattle depot on the plains. Texans wanted a safe and accessible market for the longhorn cattle, but were generally met with resistance wherever they turned.

McCoy's Great Western Stockyards provided an answer for the Texas drovers. There was lots of room for cattle to graze while they awaited sale.

In 1868, Abilene's population swelled with the new business created by the cattle industry. Many of the new arrivals were gamblers, gunmen, pimps and prostitutes.

The *Topeka Commonwealth*, in July 1868, bemoaned the happenings in Abilene:

> *"At this writing Hell is now in session in Abilene."*

The town went through two years of terror generated by shooting and shouting in from the trail. The alien cowboys openly taunted city officials.

Abilene's mayor, Theodore C. Henry, desperately sought an effective peacekeeper. Most applicants interviewed simply couldn't cope with the Texas rowdies.

When Tom "Bear River" Smith, a redheaded one hundred and seventy pound Irishman from Colorado came to apply, Mayor Henry was hardly impressed. He tried a number of other so-called peacekeepers. None could measure up to the job.

Mayor Henry was down to his last resort. He telegraphed Smith to come for the job. He was paid $150 a month. Smith's "Bear River" nickname came from battling a vigilante group in Wyoming.

Smith's first act was to enforce a city ordinance prohibiting the carrying of guns in Abilene. Big "Hank" Hawkins and the burly "Wyoming Frank" soon challenged him. Smith overpowered and disarmed both of them and then banished them from the town. The new town marshal didn't use a weapon to confront his first antagonists.

The lawman quickly brought a semblance of peace to Abilene. After capturing some Nebraska cattle rustlers, Abilene increased his salary to $225 a month.

While trying to arrest Andrew McConnell, a farmer for murdering his neighbor, Smith was wounded by a gunshot from the farmer's weapon. He was then viciously slashed and killed with an axe.

Abilene's former raucous disorder soon returned. The City of Abilene did put a permanent reminder at Smith's gravesite. It read:

Thomas J. Smith
Marshall of Abilene, 1870
Died, a martyr to Duty, Nov. 2, 1870
A Fearless Hero of Frontier Days
Who in Cowboy Chaos
Established the Supremacy of Law.

Dodge City: Fort Dodge was established in 1865 to protect the freight wagons traveling on the Santa Fe Trail from marauding Indians.

Dodge City boomed when it became a railhead for Texas cattle.
(Kansas Historical Society)

153

It wasn't until 1872 that Dodge City was born on the open prairie, five miles from Fort Dodge. In its early days Dodge City was known as "Hide Town" because of the hundreds of thousands of buffalo hides shipped each year by rail car.

When stacks of buffalo hides towered along Front Street, filthy buffalo hunters and traders filled the town's establishments and the term "stinker" was coined.

Trainmasters arriving in Dodge City would take their red caboose lanterns along when visiting the town's "soiled doves", and the term, "red light district", came to life.

Caldwell: Cowboys dubbed Caldwell as the "Border Queen". When they arrived at Caldwell, they knew they were out of Indian Territory.

During its wild days, Caldwell went through 16 marshals in six years.

By the early 1880's, just about all of Kansas was closed to drovers because of the Texas fever their cattle carried. Also, Railroads were cutting across the most remote reaches of the High Plains, making cattle ranching profitable in Colorado, Wyoming and Montana.

The Texas longhorn was no longer "King" of the western ranges.

Chapter 24

John Chisum, Cattle Baron

He had a run-in with 'Billy the Kid'

> "The noisy fellow in exaggerated costume that rode up and down the streets whooping and shooting in the air was never a cowpuncher from any outfit. He was usually some 'would-be' bad man from the East decked out in paraphernalia from Montgomery Ward's of Chicago. (Granville Stuart in 1925)

(Authors note: This John Chisum has been listed in some accounts as the Chisholm that laid out the Chisholm. This is not true. Notice the difference in the spelling. We have seen some writers (on the Internet) that have gotten the two men confused.)

John Chisum never looked back once he set his goal.

He was born in Tennessee to Claiborne and Lucinda Chisum, who were cousins. Chisum accompanied his parents and other relatives to Red River County, Texas in 1837.

Young John worked as a store clerk in Paris, Texas. He started accumulating land and operated several small grocery stores. He was a member of the I.O.O.F. lodge and held the office of Lamar county clerk from 1852-54.

Chisum filed homestead claims on land in northwestern Denton County, Texas and purchased a cattle herd with Stephen K. Fowler, a New Orleans investor. With these, he entered the cattle business with the Half Circle P brand.

A family traveling to California during the gold rush spent the night at Chisum's ranch. With them was a pretty mulatto girl, named Jensie. The family needed money and offered to sell Jensie to Chisum for fourteen hundred dollars.

A bachelor, Chisum fathered two children by Jensie. When Chisum moved his cattle operation further west, he placed

Texas longhorns on a trail drive.
(Photo by Carolyn Hunter, Texas
Longhorn Breeders Assn)

Jensie and his two daughters in a house in Bonham, Texas, and Chisum paid their upkeep. He returned to visit them on several occasions.

Chisum had a brief run-in with William "Billy the Kid" Bonney over a debt that Bonney claimed Chisum owed. Chisum refused to pay and Bonney responded by promising to steal enough cattle to make up the sum.

Billy the Kid followed through on the promise. With a gang that included Dave Rudabaugh, Billy Wilson, Tom O'Folliard and Charles Bowdre, Billy's gang became a big problem for Lincoln County cattlemen.

Lawman Pat Garrett later shot and killed both O'Folliard and Bowdre. Soon after, he captured Billy the Kid, Dave Rudabaugh and Billy Watson.

Chisum became an active cattle dealer in search of markets. Besides his own cattle, he managed the herds of neighboring families and various partners, sharing in the calves these herds produced.

He drove a small herd of cattle to a packing plant in Jefferson, Texas. By 1860, the aggressive Chisum was running five thousand head of cattle, valued at thirty five thousand dollars. He also owned six slaves

John Chisum had this portrait made in the late 1800s.

Chisum was exempted from service in the Civil War. Early in 1862, Chisum drove a herd of cattle across Arkansas to the Confederate forces at Vicksburg. After this, he showed little interest in the southern cause.

He then joined forces with Charles Goodnight to trail enough beef to feed eight thousand Navajo Indians on the Bosque Redondo Reservation near Fort Sumner, New Mexico. When the

157

government later moved the Indians to Arizona in 1868, that market vanished.

Even so, Chisum kept growing. He abandoned his Texas base and established his headquarters ranch at Bosque Grande, New Mexico.

Chisum claimed a cattle range that extended more than one hundred miles down the Pecos River. Marauding Indians crippled his operations in 1874 and he lost one hundred and fifty thousand dollars. This forced him to transfer his livestock holdings, estimated at more than sixty thousand head, to a St. Louis beef commission house.

He didn't claim to be a trail driver. Neither did he spend a great deal of time on the ranch or on the range. He was a cattle dealer that traveled in search of markets.

Chisum died of cancer at Eureka Springs, Arkansas on December 22, 1884. He was buried at Paris, Texas.

Chapter 25

The Wild Ride of F.X. Aubry

> Aubry rode hard, covering one hundred miles a day. When he arrived in Independence fourteen days later, he had beat the record set by Norris Colburn in 1846 by ten and a half days.

He was called "Little Aubry" and weighed perhaps one hundred pounds soaking wet. But he could ride!

As an adult, F.X. Aubry stood only five feet two inches tall.

Francis X. Aubry (Kansas State Historical Society)

After traveling to St. Louis, Missouri, traders assured him there was a lot of money to be made in transporting and selling trade goods in Santa Fe, New Mexico.

The diminutive Aubry secured a loan from a St. Louis firm and hired a freighting firm to transport the goods to Santa Fe. When he arrived, he found that Santa Fe was now in American hands. When Mexico attacked American troops on the southern border of Texas, General Winfield Scott occupied Mexico City and ended the war.

The U.S. annexed Texas and Mexico ceded California and New Mexico, including all the present-day states of the southwest.

Aubry sold his goods for enough money to pay off his debt. He then became involved in carrying the U.S. Mail, as well as transporting goods over the Santa Fe Trail from Missouri to Santa Fe.

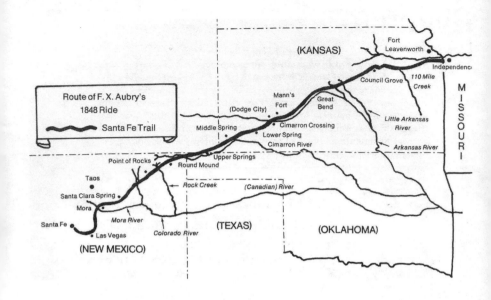

Aubry's route ran eight hundred miles.
(Kansas State Historical Society)

Government and military mail was taking at least thirty days by mule. When sent by ox teams pulling heavy freight wagons, it took sixty to ninety days.

He offered to carry the mail on a return trip from Santa Fe to Independence, Missouri, which he was making by horseback. He left Santa Fe December 22, 1847 with a party of four men and a servant. When Mexican bandits attacked the party, everybody dropped out, leaving Aubry alone. Later, he lost another ten hours fighting off some Indians.

Aubry rode hard, covering one hundred miles a day. When he arrived in Independence fourteen days later, he had beat the record set by Norris Colburn in 1846 by ten and a half days.

Little Aubry wasn't satisfied. He was sure he could make the ride in eight days.

Bettors lined up to place their money on Little Aubry's wild ride. Aubry, himself, bet one thousand dollars that he could beat

160

his previous record. In fact, he bet that he could complete the ride from Santa Fe to Independence within six days.

He was better prepared for this ride. He sent men ahead with fresh horses and had then stationed all along his route.

He left Santa Fe at a full gallop for the ride of his life on September 12, 1848. He changed horses at various stops along the way. When he neared Point Reyes early in the morning. His favorite mare, "Dolly" was waiting for him.

Even in the rain, this small mare of Spanish blood didn't slow down. He rode Dolly one hundred miles before he planned to get a new mount. As he approach the station where he would change horses, instead of a new mount, he found a dead man that had been scalped by Indians.

The Indians had also run off the horses. He would ride Dolly another one hundred miles before he finding a wagon train with horses.

Dolly had set a record, traveling two hundred miles at a speed of eight miles an hour over a twenty-six hour period.

At ten o'clock at night September 17, Little Aubry pulled up in front of the Merchant's Hotel in Independence. He was weak but alive. Men rushed out to help him from the saddle.

He had won his bet, making the ride from Santa Fe to Independence in five days and sixteen hours.

In 1853, fortune played a cruel trip on the little rider. This event occurred in 1853 when Aubry was taking ten wagons filled with merchandise from Santa Fe to the gold fields of California.

Aubry kept a meticulous diary of his trips. On August 3, 1853 he wrote:

> *Indians shooting arrows around us all day wounded some of our mules and my famous mare, Dolly, who has so often rescued me from danger by her speed and capacity for endurance."*

On August 16, after being wounded eight times, and he and his men were on half rations of horsemeat, Aubry added another entry to his diary:

> *"I have the misfortune to know that the flesh we are eating is that of my inestimable mare Dolly who so often saved me from death at the hands of Indians. She gave out on account of her wounds."*

A year later, Little Aubry himself was stabbed to death while at a *cantina* in Santa Fe.

Chapter 26

Mavericks

> With lots of cowboys in his pay;
> He Old Diamond Joe was a rich old jay,
> rode the range with his cowboy band,
> And many a mav'rick got his brand.
> ("Diamond Joe" in Lomax's *Cowboy Songs*)

A maverick was a calf that was missed during the roundup process and since weaned from its mother.

There was no way of telling who owned it. That, however, didn't stop a lot of people from throwing their own brand on such animals and adding them to their own herds.

One story says the term "maverick" derived from Samuel Maverick, a Texas businessman. He left four hundred head of cattle behind when he moved from Matagorda to San Antonio. When these cattle reproduced, the offspring were not branded and pretty much roamed at will.

Charles Siringo, a cowboy turned author, relates this story in an autobiography. *Samuel Maverick*, he said, "being a chickenhearted old rooster, wouldn't brand or earmark any of his cattle."

All his neighbors, however, branded not only their own, but Mavericks, as well. Eventually, anyone seeing an unbranded animal would say, "Yonder goes one of Mr. Maverick's animals." Later, anyone seeing an unbranded animal anywhere, people would say, "Yonder goes a maverick."

Still another version, also told by Siringo, happened at a stock growers meeting in Texas. Each man declared publicly what brand and earmark he would use. Finally, the story goes, everyone but an "old Longhorn named Maverick" had recorded his brand.

He said he didn't intend to use any brand at all, and that when other ranchers saw anything unbranded, they would know it belonged to him—"and would please not claim it."

A cowboy ropes a maverick. (from "The Longhorns" by J. Frank Dobie)

Some historians say that by 1861, Samuel Maverick was the largest landholder in the United States and owned more cattle than any other man in Texas. His ambition, it was said, was to be able to travel from San Antonio to El Paso, all on his own land, and to stock that land with cattle.

Still another tale says that Maverick had his cattle on Matagorda Island off the coast of Texas. As they were cut off from all other cattle, Maverick didn't have to bother branding them. One night, however, a summer storm came raging through and blew all the water out of the pass between the island and the mainland. The cattle rushed across, mixed with other cattle, and were dispersed beyond recovery.

Mavericks provided a real temptation to someone who wanted to get into the cattle business without laying out a great deal of money.

Cattle barons (they hated this name) weren't guiltless. In the days when the herds were being gathered after the civil war, large ranchers had a tendency to brand anything not already branded.

This Texas system of branding every yearling found without a brand soon reached the northern plains. In their book, "The American Cowboy," Joe B. Frantz and Julian Ernest Choate, Jr., write: "It was an axiom that an outfit never ate its own beef if a neighbor's was available."

Uninformed people sometimes confuse "maverick" with "dogie". A dogie may become a maverick if not found and branded. The term, however, refers to an orphaned calf left on its own.

A brand pretty much identifies an animal for all future time. A brand won't rub off or wear off. It won't be lost or mislaid. Brands are on record with each state and can easily be traced if the brand is not readily identified.

This doesn't mean that brands could not be changed and altered. They often were by clever rustlers that were virtual artists with a running iron or D-ring in their hands.

Consider how a simple brand can be changed. A rancher with a **C C** brand might someday discover that some of his cattle had disappeared. They were now wearing a **Bar 8 8.**

Brands are usually read from top to bottom and from left to right. Horizontal lines are bars; diagonal lines are slashes; while vertical lines are either ones or I's. Curved lines are quarter circles and half circles, but can also serve as "rockers" or "swings".

There is one story about cowboys wooing Lilybell, the daughter of a rancher. In attempts to impress the young lady, the smitten cowboys would burn **LIL** on any mavericks they found on the range.

Eventually, the number of animals bearing **LIL** grew large enough that Lilybell registered the brand and went into the cattle business for herself.

Cowboy historian J. Frank Dobie tells a story that emphasizes the importance of a brand.

A twenty-year-old cowboy named Adolph Huffmeyer was working for thirty dollars a month branding mavericks for his employer. He decided he could do the same thing on his own and be a cattleman himself.

Huffmeyer had saved a little money. He bought three horses, a supply of coffee, salt and meal, and a can to boil the coffee in. He took a skillet for making corn bread, his overcoat, which was not rainproof, two blankets, a running iron and an extra rope, and began camping out where the dry cattle ran.

He figured if he could average six mavericks a day, he would soon have a nice little herd.

For his brand, he decided to use the year he was starting his newfound business, **7 T 6** —"Seventy six." His earmark was a smooth crop on the right ear and an under half crop on the left.

After six weeks, a cowboy friend of Huffmeyer's said, "Of course, you've got that brand and mark recorded."

Not knowing much about records, Huffmeyer was waiting on the courthouse steps at daylight to record his brand with the county clerk.

"What brand do you want to record," the clerk asked.

"**7 T 6**" Huffmeyer said, scrawling it on a piece of paper.

The clerk opened his brand book and scanned the pages. "Why, just the other day, so-and-so recorded **7 T 6** as his brand with the very same earmark you give."

Huffmeyer had just branded two hundred fifty cattle for another man.

It is said that some illegitimate "maverickers" would slit the tongue of a sucking calf so that it could no longer suck and would stop following its mother. A calf with a slit tongue would not bawl for its mother.

What ever happened to Samuel Maverick?

In 1856, he sold out his stock of cattle, which he estimated at four hundred head, for six dollars each, range delivery. The purchaser, Toutrant Beauregard, bought the animals "as they ran." If there were more than four hundred head, he was the gainer for his purchase; if less, he was the loser.

The term "maverick" generated in a soft synonym for stealing. It is no longer a term a respectable cowboy wants pinned on him.

Chapter 27

The Bosses

> Calamity Jane walked in. Teddy Blue had met her before. He told her, "I'll give you two dollars and a half if you'll go and sit on his lap and kiss him."

The cowboys revered some trail bosses, but there were others who brought the morale of the cowboys to the lowest point possible.

"Teddy" Blue Abbott saw them all, but he was especially down on one in particular. This was a man who was manager and part owner of the **F U F** outfit. "What he didn't know about a trail herd would make a book so big you couldn't load it on a flatcar with a block and tackle," said Abbott.

"He fed a lot of cattle in Nebraska on corn, but he didn't know a cowpuncher when he saw one, and he hired everybody that came along. There was only three or four good cowboys in the outfit, counting myself as one," Abbott bemoaned.

The others, he said, "Didn't know enough to pull on a rope."

Abbott described the cattle boss as a man who was a pious New Englander that would say his prayers at night and then give a cowpuncher ten dollars the next day to steal a calf. Aside from that, said Abbott, half the orders he gave were wrong.

The cowboy cited the instance when he was sent to Fort Kearney by train to help bring back a load of horses. The boss ordered that all of the rail cars be bedded with straw instead of sand because straw was cheaper.

While going up a grade against the wind, sparks from the engine set the front car on fire. The cowboys back in the caboose didn't discover the fire for a while, and when they did, couldn't get the engineer to stop.

"I was running along over the top of the train toward the engine, shooting at the bell with my six-shooter. The engineer finally caught on that something was wrong. We finally got the horses out as soon as we could, but I never want to see anything like that again. Some had their eyes burned out, and all their hair was gone, and blood was coming out of their nostrils with every breath," Abbott recalled in his book, "We Pointed Them North."

Calamity Jane

"We were going to shoot them, but the old man (trail boss) wouldn't let us. He said if we shot them he might not be able to collect his damages from the railroad company. We had to go off and leave them there. The man in charge of the second train shot them when he came along."

Abbott did get some satisfaction from playing a trick on the trail boss, with the help of Calamity Jane during a stop in Miles City, Montana.

The trail boss had issued orders forbidding his cowboys from bringing the *Police Gazette* to the ranch. While on the trail, he ordered the men not to take a drink. At Miles City, the boss was sitting in the hotel lobby, where he could keep his eye on the bar and see that none of his boys was in there.

Calamity Jane walked in. Teddy Blue had met her before. He told her, "I'll give you two dollars and a half if you'll go and sit on his lap and kiss him."

Teddy Blue added, "And she was game. She walked up to him with everybody watching her, and sat down on his lap and threw both arms around him so his arms were pinned to his sides and he couldn't help himself—she was as strong as a bear. And then she began kissing him and saying: "Why don't you ever come to see me any more, honey?""

Teddy recalled, "The old man sputtered and spit and wiped his mouth on his handkerchief. And he left the hotel and that was the last we saw of him that night."

Chapter 28

A Sense of Smell

As he neared the previous night's encampment, he spotted the black cow coming toward him. She had caught wind of her calf.

Drawing from "The Longhorns" by J. Frank Dobie

Longhorns could smell trouble. J. Frank Dobie said in his book, "The Longhorns," that like the buffalo, longhorns had an innate sense of smell. They hardly relied on their eyes for warning. Buffalos could scent a man or other enemy two miles, sometimes four miles away if they were standing on the windward side.

John Farrington, with the **J A** Ranch was part of a cattle roundup in which a big black cow was in the herd. One night, she gave birth to a calf. The newborn's legs were too wobbly to keep up with the herd.

Normally, it was the chuck wagon cook's job to put a newborn calf into his wagon. This time, the cook failed to do so. When Farrington saw the calf was missing from the black cow's side, he rode back for it.

He found it where the mother cow had left it. Farrington lifted it up and placed it in the saddle in front of him. When he got back to the herd, the cowboys had tired of trying to keep the mother cow with the herd and left her go back in search of her offspring.

Farmington then doubled back with the calf still in front of him, determined to get the two together. As he neared the previous night's encampment, he spotted the black cow coming toward him. She had caught wind of her calf.

The cow followed him back to the herd where she finally regained her baby.

Cattlemen used various devices to keep mothers and babies together in the cattle herds. If several calves were in the chuck wagon bed at the same time, their smell became mixed, confusing the mothers, who sometimes refused to accept them.

Trail boss Charles Goodnight resorted to placing newborn calves inside a loose gunnysack as they rode in the chuck wagon. When the herd bedded down, the calves were released and each mother readily knew her calf by smell.

The most dangerous enemy of cattle on the open range was the wolf, not the coyote. The coyote would seldom attack even the tiniest calf and never a full-grown animal, but the lobo, which roved in bands, could bring down a large bull in a buffalo herd.

Goodnight also used a clever technique to get a mother cow to accept a strange calf. If a cow lost her calf and at the same time there was a calf that had lost its mother, the bloodless hide of the dead calf, fastened loosely over the orphan, would influence the cow to adopt it.

By milking some of the cow's milk onto the head of the orphan, the adoption process was hastened.

James J. Hollister, Sr, son of Col. W.W. Hollister, founder of the town of Hollister, California supervised Rancho Refugio, near Santa Barbara. He used a Mexican technique to lure critters from the chaparral-choked canyons on the ranch. This technique worked on the cattle's sense of smell and was known as the "bloody hide" method.

It was a method supposedly invented by the Ortegas and involved the placement of a hide from a freshly butchered bull over a bush. The odor of the fresh hide drew bellowing cattle like a magnet from the brushy hillsides without the need of vaqueros.

There is evidence that cattle can smell water from four to ten miles away, when on a cross or adverse wind.

Cowboy Jack Potter told J. Frank Dobie about driving a herd over an eighty-mile dry stretch from Fort Sumner to Thatcher, Colorado. The cowherd was in great distress, and as far as Potter knew, it was still forty miles to water.

He noticed a lead steer, which he had named "Sid Boykin", lift its head, smell along, and then headed east.

When "Old Sid" headed east, Potter told his crew, "I'm going to ride in the direction he's pointed. If I find water, I'll signal you to bring the herd."

After riding for about a half-hour, Potter saw wild mustangs and antelope and knew there must be water in the area. About seven miles from where "Old Sid" had sniffed, Potter found a solitary lake of clear fresh water, surrounded by grass.

He camped his cattle there for three days while they filled up on grass and fresh water.

Chapter 29

Hardships on Women

> If we seek the prairie it is an open plain, without a shade or rock or even a hill to hide us from the gaze of a noisy company."

The rigors of traveling to get to the west were a true hardship on women. It wasn't the grueling wagons, but the lack of privacy the women missed.

Sarah Smith wrote to relatives: "One thing I greatly desire of which I must be deprived, that is retirement. The tent with the two families is the only place for prayers. If we seek the prairie it is an open plain, without a shade or rock or even a hill to hide us from the gaze of a noisy company."

Some of the women were as important, or more so, in settling the west as were the men.

Mary Fields

Mary Fields was born a slave in Tennessee in 1832 and grew up to be an orphan. She never married. Mary lived by her wits and by her strength.

She traveled to Ohio and settled in Toledo, where she worked in a Catholic convent. She formed a strong bond with Mother Amadeus. The nuns then moved to Montana. When Mary learned of Mother Amadeus' failing health, she rushed to help out.

Mary was hired to do "heavy work" and to haul freight and supplies to keep the nuns' operation going. She helped the nuns build the St. Peter's mission school and was devout in her protection of the nuns. She was described as a pistol packing, hard-drinking woman, who needed nobody to fight her battles.

When Mary was turned away from the mission because of her behavior, the nuns financed Mary in her own business.

Mary opened a cafe. Her cooking was rather basic and not the most appetizing, and her customers dwindled to the point that Mary had to close.

Eventually, Mary found a job that suited her. In 1895, she became a U.S. mail coach driver for the Cascade County region of central Montana.

Her reputation for carrying mail in any kind of weather grew. Mary would ride through freezing winters or blistering heat to get the mail to the remote miner's cabins and other outposts in the region. She and her mule, Moses, never missed a day, and it was in this capacity that Mary earned the nickname of "Stagecoach".

She continued in this capacity until she was into her sixties but her age finally forced her to retire. Still needing income, at the age of seventy, Mary opened a laundry service in Cascade, Montana.

Nancy Judson

It required an act of the legislature for a woman to get a divorce in Oregon Territory. The following petition recounts the poor treatment that Nancy Judson received from her husband. Her plea for divorce is printed just as she wrote it in 1858.

Polk County O.T. Nov. 15 Ad 1858

I humbly beg of the Legislator of oregon to grant me a bill of divorcement for I cannot live with Mr. Judson he misuses me in every shape he is capable of doing he has knocked me down and scolded me and beemeaned me in everry shape and lyed on me as bad as any one could lly on another and does not Provide for me Nor the family as he aught to do But has squandered all that father has givin mee and has mortgaged my land and his and it is all gone and he is not able to support me nor the Children neither is he capable of taking care of us the children are ragged and go not fit to bee seen and have to depend on the Neigbors for their bread and do not get mutch of that I have not lived with Mr Judson since the first of last December Ad 1857 from that time to this I have had to support my self as best I could and the children has been Poorly taken care of for they have had to take care of them selves in a maner that is too of them I have one them with me sending him to school the youngest a little boy the other too is down at Clatsap wher he keeps them half stalved and half naked My Children has never been to school of an consiquenc and e nevere will sene them I have three children one little girl 10 years olde the 10 day of next december one boy 12 years olde 22 of February next the youngest is alittle boy 7 years olde the 26 day of may next and he knows more than all the rest for I have been sendding him to school ever since wee parted Now if it will please your honerble boddy to give me a bill and give me the Children I will every Pray ec

I ever remain your humble friend
Mrs. Nancy Judson

The legislature granted Mrs. Judson a divorce.

Elizabeth Williams

Elizabeth Ellen Johnson Williams established herself in the west by teaching school and working part-time as a bookkeeper for cattlemen. While doing her bookkeeping chores, Lizzie learned about the profits to be made in the cattle business. In 1871, she registered her own brand under the name, Elizabeth Johnson.

Two days later she made her first real-estate transaction by purchasing ten acres of land in Austin, Texas, from Charles W.

179

Whitis, one of the cattlemen for whom she kept books. She paid Whitis three thousand gold dollars for the property.

Elizabeth soon became known as a Texas "cattle queen" because of her cattle investments. She is thought to be the first woman to ride the Chisholm Trail with a herd of cattle she had acquired under her own brand.

She married Hezekiah G. Williams in 1879. She insisted the coupled sign a pre-marital agreement that would allow her to retain control of her financial affairs and keep her property separate.

Her husband died in1914, and Lizzie grew increasingly reclusive and eccentric. She developed a reputation for being miserly, and appeared to the outside world, to be impoverished.

People in Austin were startled to learn after her death that Lizzie had amassed almost quarter million dollars. Her holdings included property in Travis, Llano, Hays, Trinity, Culberson, and Jeff Davis counties.

Nellie Cashman

When Nellie Cashman was working as a bellhop in a prominent Boston hotel, she met General Ulysses S. Grant. He urged her to go west.

Nellie took his advice. With her meager savings, Nellie, along with her sister Fannie, traveled to San Francisco. The year was 1869 and within a year Fannie married and started raising a family. Nellie took a job as a cook in various Nevada mining camps, including Virginia City and Pioche.

A gold strike in the remote Cassiar District near Juneau, Alaska attracted Nellie. She joined a group of two hundred Nevada miners headed to the Cassiar gold strike at Dease Lake, British Columbia.

Nellie earned a reputation as an angel during the winter of 1874-75. While on a trip to Victoria to purchase supplies, a winter blizzard slammed into Cassiar, cutting off the stranded miners.

Nellie purchased the supplies and sleds she needed to launch a rescue mission. She then sailed to Fort Wrangell, Alaska, with six men she had hired and headed toward Cassiar through heavy snows.

It took seventy-five days for Nellie and her group to reach Cassiar. Her success in reaching the miners with the needed medicine and food became the talk of the west.

Mary never struck it rich with all her chasing of silver and gold strikes. She finally decided, in 1879, to head for the warm climate of Arizona Territory. There she opened a restaurant in Tucson. Within a year, she moved on to Tombstone, where again she opened a restaurant.

When asked why she never married, Nellie replied, "I haven't had time for marriage. Men are nuisances. They're just boys grown up. I've nursed them, embalmed them, fed and scolded them, acted as mother confessor and fought my own with them and you have to treat them just like boys."

Nellie finally settled down in Victoria, British Columbia. She died January 25, 1925 as she approached her eightieth birthday.

Chapter 30

Prairie Fires

> *"I was fighting fire with all my might, whipping it with my old slicker until midnight."*

A range fire's greatest threat was in its swiftness. High winds usually accompanied such events. Range fires have been recorded traveling up to eight miles and hour.

A range fire was a fearsome spectacle for cowboys and cattle alike.
(From watercolor by Richard Schlecht)

The range fire cannot only run, but it can jump. It's known to leap a river one hundred-seventy-feet wide.

John Leakey, six-foot-six-foot Texan, described how cowboys battled a Montana grass fire in the book, "The American Cowboy, In Life and Legend": "I was fighting fire with all my might, whipping it with my old slicker until midnight."

Three days later, the fire had scorched fifty thousand acres in spite of the fire-fighting efforts of fifty men.

To fight the fires, cowboys killed a steer to use as a fire drag. They picked the biggest animal available, skinned out half the carcass, and refilled it with dirt. The backbone of the dead animal kept the hide stretched out when a cowboy, with a lariat tied to the front and rear legs, dragged it around the perimeter of the fire.

When a pioneer saw that long band of red light in the distance, he jumped to action, even though the firebreak plowed around his property might act as a small barrier against the wildfire.

The settler hurriedly made firebrands from hazel brush lit them and began starting backfires. The inner edge of the fire facing his crops or house was beaten out and the outside of the fire was allowed to burn toward the oncoming wildfire.

It was fire fighting against fire. The settler's strategy usually worked. He would watch as the fiery monster changed course.

Lightening started many prairie fires. Native American tribes set prairie fires, knowing that the fires would burn away the dead and dying vegetation. Some tribes set fires to assist them in hunting. The fires drove the wild game toward waiting hunting parties.

Prairie fires were a major deterrent to white settlers venturing out onto the open plains.

Chapter 31

Frontier Courtroom

> *"Trot out the wicked and unfortunate, and let the cotillion commence," said his Honor.*

During Dodge City's heydey as a cowtown, the courtroom provided the only theatrical stage that small settlements had. The legal wranglings and goings on were true theater in some of them.

This account was printed in the *Dodge City Times*, August 11, 1877:

> *"The Marshal will preserve strict order," said the judge. "Any person caught throwing turnips, cigar stumps, beets, or old quids of tobacco in this Court, will be immediately arranged before this bar of Justice." Then Joe (a local policeman) looked savagely at the mob in attendance, hitched his ivory handle a little to the left and adjusted his moustache.*
>
> *"Trot out the wicked and unfortunate, and let the cotillion commence," said his Honor.*
>
> *City vs. James Martin—But just then a complaint not on file had to be attended to, and Reverend John Walsh of Los Animas, took the Throne of Justice, while the Judge stepped over to Hoover's (a saloon).*

"You are here for horse stealing," says Walsh.

"I can clean out the damned court," says Martin. *Then the City Attorney was banged into a pigeonhole in the desk, the table upset, the windows kicked out and the railing broke down. When order was restored, Joe's thumb was "some chawed," Assistant Marshal Ed Masterson's nose sliced a trifle, and the cantankerous originator of all this, James Martin, Esq., was bleeding from a half dozen cuts on his head, inflicted by Masterson's revolver. Then Walsh was deposed and Judge Frost took his set, chewing burnt coffee, as his habit, for his complexion. The evidence was brief and pointed.*

"Again," said the Judge, as he rested his alabaster brow on his left paw, "do you appear within this sacred realm, of which I, and only I am high muck-i-muck. You have disturbed the quiet of our lovely village. Why, instead of letting the demon of passion fever your brain into this fray, did you not shake hands and call it all a mistake. When the lion and the lamb would have lain down together and white-robed peace would have fanned you with her silvery wings and elevate your thoughts to the good and pure by her smiles of approbation; but no you went to chawing and clawing and pulling hair. It is $10.00 and costs, Mr. Martin."

A Texas judge handed down the following sentence, which is unedited from the original version:

> *"The fact is Jones, the court did not intend to order you to be executed before next spring, but being as the weather is cold and the jail is in such miserable shape, with much of the glass broken, and owing to the great amount of prisoners already in the jail and considering the hardships it would impose on the sheriff to have to look after you until next spring and considering the fact that there are not enough blankets for all the prisoners I feel as if you would undoubtedly not be comfortable in such surroundings.*
>
> *"Therefore it is the order of the court, that in order to alleviate your sufferings and provide the compassionate care a man in your present situation requires, that you should be hung as soon as possible tomorrow morning when the sheriff has finished his breakfast or as soon as possible thereafter."*

The famous Judge Roy Bean dished out the following sentence:

Jose Manuel Miguel Gonzales, in a few short weeks it will be spring.
The snows of winter will flow away, the ice will vanish, the air will become soft and balmy.
The annual mircle (sic) of the years will awaken and come to pass.

The rivulet will run its soaring course to the sea.

The timid desert flowers will put fourth their tender shoots.

The glorious valleys of this imperial domain will blossom as the rose.

Judge Roy Bean

From every treetop, some wild songster will carol his mating song.

Butterflies will sport in the sunshine.

But you will not be their (sic) to enjoy it. Because I command the sheriff of the county to lead you away to some remote spot, swing you by the neck from a knotting bough of some sturdy oak and let you hang until dead.

And then Jose Manuel Miguel Gonzales, I further command that such officers retire quickly from your dangling corpse, that vultures may descend from the heavens upon your filthy body until nothing is left but the bare, bleached bones of a cold-blooded, blood-thirsty, throat-cutting, mudering (sic) S.O.B.

Index

About the Author

Alton Pryor has been a writer for magazines, newspapers, and wire services. He worked for United Press International in their Sacramento Bureau, handling both printed press as well as radio news.

He then moved to Salinas, where he worked for the Salinas Californian daily newspaper for five years as editor of Western Ranch and Home, a weekend supplement.

In 1963, he joined California Farmer magazine where he worked as a field editor for 27 years. When that magazine was sold, the new owners forced him into retirement, which was too soon for the still active writer.

He gained an intense interest in California history after selling a number of short 500-word articles on Southern California history. In his research of these stories, he kept running across other stories that interested him but did not fit the particular publication for whom he was then writing. He began collecting both facts and ideas as he researched, and finally turned them into his first book, "Little Known Tales in California History."

Alton Pryor is now the author of eleven books, "Little Known Tales in California History," "Classic Tales in California History," "Those Wild and Lusty Gold Camps," "California's Hidden Gold," "Outlaws and Gunslingers," "Historic California, It's Colorful Names and How It Got Them," "Jonathan's Red Apple Tree," a children's book, , "Publish It Yourself: Five Easy Steps to Getting Your Book into Print," "Little Known Tales in Nevada History," and his newest book, "Little Known Tales in Hawaii History."

He is a graduate of California State Polytechnic University, San Luis Obispo, where he earned a Bachelor of Science degree in journalism.